Delight

An Enchanted Self Book

By

Dr. Barbara Becker Holstein

authorHOUSE™

1663 LIBERTY DRIVE, SUITE 200
BLOOMINGTON, INDIANA 47403
(800) 839-8640
WWW.AUTHORHOUSE.COM

First published by AuthorHouse 04/18/05

ISBN: 1-4208-2554-2 (sc)

Printed in the United States of America
Bloomington, Indiana

This book is printed on acid-free paper.

The Enchanted Self® is a registered trademark of Barbara Becker Holstein

This book is an Enchanted Self Book. It is Volume II of the Wisdom and Wonder Collection for Women. Volume I is **Feel Good Stories** by Bernice Becker.

www.enchantedself.com

What People Are Saying...

Taking a title from one of her stories, Mazal Tov, I tip my hat to Dr. Holstein. She does have a job to do - to provide joy - and she accomplished that goal in such a delightful book. May we all grow, learn, and live each day in a positive way - as she guides each of us on our own journey - wherever it may lead.

~Frieda Resnick, Israel

After reading her book, I felt not only inspired but also intrigued by her journey toward joy and Delight. Dr. Holstein weaves the stories in such a way, that I could relate to them easily. I felt that my story was somehow intermingled with her stories. Not only did I read stories of traditions that I am not familiar with, I also got to know the "real" Barbara as a warm, caring and intuitive person who's life goal is to help others reclaim their Enchanted Self.

~Karin Janin, Author 'Magic of Intent'

Dr Barbara Becker Holstein has put together a remarkable collection of uplifting stories that will inspire you to enchantment. Reading her spiritual journey back to her Jewish roots was really motivating!

Why wait for an unhappy occasion? Begin your search today with Barbara Becker Holstein. This book is sure to inspire to begin your own search for Delight.

Dr. Barbara Becker Holstein's sharing of her Judaic journey, from somewhat affiliated to fully involved, is both sensitive and charming. Tidbits of psychological observations smoothly meld in with the personal tales of Holstein and others, touching on all facets of Jewish traditions, holidays, and everyday wonders of enchantment. A fast-paced attention grabbing read for a pleasant afternoon!

Did you miss out on traditions when you were a kid? No problem, Dr. Holstein, author of **DELIGHT**, takes you by the hand and lovingly shows you how it is never too late to connect with your traditions.

Over many years as an observant Jew I came to take certain things for granted and forgot some of the warm wonderful feeling of belonging I experienced at the start of my journey. Thank you so much for putting me in touch with these memories.

~Tsipa Esther, NYC

Dr. Holstein's book helps others to reflect, providing a new pathway to see themselves. Mazel Tov!

~Cindy Costa, New Jersey

The message that Dr. Holstein portrays in her stories is meaningful and should help bring thousands of readers, both young and old, to a greater inspiration of life and family.

~Rabbi Yosef Carlebach, Director, Chabad House, Rutgers University Campus

Please read *DELIGHT* with an open heart and mind on a train, in bed, anywhere and discover your 'ache' for spiritual nourishment. I could not put the book down; each chapter fed my Enchanted Self.

~Roger King, Author "Love The Miracle Your Are" & Making Love with Passionate Thoughts."

Barbara's personal assignments at the end of her stories allow us to be part of her quest. We can find our similarities to her experiences and our differences. It does not matter. After all, we are all unique.

~Ellen Saposnick, Educator, Florida

DEDICATION

This book is a tribute to my mother-in-law, Mrs. Lillian Holstein, who passed away in 2000. May her soul rest in peace!

Mom shared her memories of Shabbos, with newspapers put down on Friday's newly washed wooden floors and the smells of challah and mandel bread wafting down the hallways and out into the street. Her stories, tales of New York's Lower East Side, included the wedding that took place in her building with several apartments opening their doors to make the whole floor a wedding hall for the day. Her philanthropic work included her service as International President of B'nai B'rith Women, her many trips to Israel, her important work helping oppressed Jewish communities around the world, and her love for the B'nai B'rith Treatment Center in Jerusalem for boys with special needs. All of her sharing represented sparks of energy, commitment, and strength of character that made her an indelibly extraordinary person to countless people.

Mom, I want you to know that your example, your philosophy, and your joie de vivre truly penetrated. I offer **DELIGHT** as one of the ways that I can pass on some of the energy that I received from you to the world. Thank you, Mom. I will never forget you!

✗

For Everyone There Comes a Time for Delight

This is the time when we come home
To the parts of ourselves lost long ago,
When we let the door open
And allow the positive to resonate . . .

When we permit the incubation of pleasure,
Sure that we are imbued with our own
Special dignity and voice,

When we travel roads both familiar and not,
Climb mountains, bathe in pure waters,
Seek lost traditions, and make new ones.

It takes will to overcome darkness and pursue,
But we know that our souls need this nourishment.

For each of us, it happens—our lost potential is revived.
We find paths that fit our footprints—Needs finally met,
Rituals, Celebrations Galore, and of course,

Delight!

Table of Contents

A STEP BACK IN TIME
A Hole in My Heart

I had been feeling low. Of course, we all have our moments of feeling down and discouraged, but I was having trouble making any sense of mine. I felt a gnawing mental malaise, an emotional hole in my heart. Something was definitely missing.

In many ways I was on top of the world. I had finally finished rigorous training as a private-practice psychologist, passed my exams, and was in full-time practice with my husband. I had fascinating clients; my two children were growing and thriving. We traveled, I was in good health, I was fairly attractive, and I had enough money for our needs.

My sad feelings persisted, however, and I wasn't sure why. Maybe I was in emotional overload from seeing so many clients and listening to problems without giving myself enough time to be with friends and family. Still, I'd devoted so many years to my professional development that I couldn't imagine spending less time at work.

Something had to be done, but I didn't know what. My husband wisely suggested that, since I seemed to be so curious about the effect of negative messages in women's lives, perhaps I should interview women who were not in my practice about the effects of negative messages on their lives. This would serve to widen my base of information and let me get to know women in a way that would take me beyond the treatment room.

It was clear that, as had my clients, I had internalized the negative messages from family and from the community at large that we all pick up in childhood.

We brainstormed, and I developed an interview-based research study. Targeting women over 35 years of age, I asked 18 women to meet me individually and respond to my questionnaire, which incorporated questions about the impact of negative messages, particularly those received during childhood. I included questions about negative messages that women may currently receive at home and at work. Almost as an afterthought, to balance the negative experiences I anticipated hearing about, I also asked them, "When do you feel most whole? When are you most happy?"

The women I interviewed were a delight. I met them in their homes, in restaurants and diners, and in my own home. They opened up to me, they cared, and they shared.

One of the first things I noticed was that the hole in my heart was getting smaller. Just from listening to so many women tell me their stories, I felt less alone. It was clear that they all had a capacity, in varying degrees, for enjoying life. They were able to experience the sense of being "right on", and they seemed connected to a fiber of living that was stimulating and sustaining. They were able to override even their most internalized, negative messages and to enjoy life in unique ways.

One day I was sitting in my sunny kitchen drinking a cup of tea and reading the interview transcripts. Time passed unnoticed. Suddenly, a phrase floated into my head: "The Disenchanted Forest, The Enchanted Self."

The phrase took on life and meaning. It wouldn't leave my mind. What these women had in common was that, even though they had grown up with some degree of disenchantment—even though they had been disappointed, criticized, hurt, thwarted, and sometimes even ridiculed— each woman had an "Enchanted Self" that managed to emerge despite her limitations.

These women had found their particular ways to be whole, maybe not all the time, but at least part of the time. While some found their salvation in healthy diets, others used humor, and still others chose to be creative and inventive.

I saw this repeatedly among the 18 women. There were those who did volunteer work and loved it, women who were raising their children in much more loving environments than they themselves had personally experienced, and women who were serving as mentors at work. Their feelings of increased happiness and self-worth permitted them to reach out to help others, despite any deficits they themselves might have suffered in their pasts.

In fact, some of the women were enjoying pastimes and pleasures that had actually derived from their dysfunctional childhoods. I was fascinated by the ways that they had found to reinvent themselves. They had taken the survival tactics they'd learned in childhood and turned them into a means of bringing pleasure into their lives and into the lives of others.

The insight that women have the capacity for the gift of enchantment became the foundation of my psychological work. I became convinced that many women, myself included, can't always explain the joyous part of their lives, nor do we always receive validation for them. Nevertheless, they exist and are there for the taking.

Rather than claim our joy, however, we forfeit it. We compromise. We feel depleted, discouraged, criticized, and tired. Feeling disappointed, both in life and in ourselves, we trudge through life tiredly and in emotional overload. Then, at some point, we stop distinguishing between the negative messages we tell ourselves and those that others tell us. We are a mess, emotionally speaking.

At the same time, we often forego the opportunities we have to gain self-knowledge, by ignoring the stories of our own lives. We tend to use our memories for retrieving negative information about ourselves and for validating disappointments and failures rather than successes. We forget or simply haven't been taught how to use our memories to retrieve and hold onto our unique precious talents, our earlier strengths, our marvelous coping skills, and our dreams. We don't realize that our lost potential can be revived, and with it, our happiness.

These women helped to give me a working definition of becoming whole that has become the core of THE ENCHANTED SELF®. THE ENCHANTED SELF, then, is a person's capacity, unique and perfectly suited to herself, to achieve positive states of well-being.

As the theory of THE ENCHANTED SELF emerged, I diligently did the same homework that I asked my clients and workshop participants to do. I looked into my own history, seeking to know myself—my positive self—better, and I discovered the most incredible things. Not only was I recalling what had always given me pleasure and joy but I was also feeling better about myself!

It was wonderful. I was feeling better emotionally, and my clients were progressing and reporting good news about themselves and their behaviors. By incorporating THE ENCHANTED SELF approach so that I could use it with my clients, I found that I, myself, had better mental armor and better weapons to fight off criticisms and deprecating remarks, whether they came from others or from my own head. I was taking risks to redefine myself in new ways, and I was becoming more comfortable with who I was. I felt somewhat like a female warrior, guided into the battle for a happier life by the strengths I had regained from my enchanted past.

One part of me was still muted—the woman with a heritage and traditions. With that part muted, my birthright to live a life of joy and meaning could not be fully reclaimed. With that part muted, delight was still not a given. With that part muted, I could not fully celebrate and love the woman I truly am.

This is the story of me reclaiming myself. That's what this book is all about. This book documents my journey into the energy, magic, and joy of returning to my Jewish heritage and the benefits gained from the spiritual and emotional infusions I received. I hope my journey serves to encourage and inspire you, whatever your background and traditions. If a part of you needs to return to your roots or to discover a new "home" to come to, I wish you the strength to do so. I guarantee that the door will open as wide for you as it did for me. It may and probably will not be the same door I went through, but it will open and receive you. This is a book, therefore, for all women, no matter what your heritage and traditions may be. My personal stories are interwoven with ponderings, journaling space, and activities to help you reclaim your own beautiful self, based on my work as a positive psychologist utilizing ENCHANTED SELF techniques.

No one should ever have to live with a hole in her heart. Yes, there comes a time in every woman's life for DELIGHT!

A TRIP TO AMISH COUNTRY
A Way Back to Myself Emerges...

It was an autumn day, crisp and sunny. The leaves were vibrant. A weekend in the Amish country seemed to be the ideal plan for the upcoming Columbus Day Weekend. I called for a room at a Mennonite farmhouse. When Mrs. Olsen answered, I imagined her standing in a whitewashed kitchen, looking out at a pasture where cows grazed. I envisioned an old fashioned, white clapboard farmhouse with wash swinging in the breeze on the lines in the backyard. I couldn't wait to make the reservation! Imagine my disappointment when Mrs. Olsen told me that they were already full for Columbus Day weekend. I had called a little too late.

I was about to hang up and was feeling very sad that I would never get to see this clapboard house with the wash blowing in the breeze, when she suddenly said to me, "Wait! Let me think about this. I think you could have our bedroom. Also, I have one small bedroom upstairs that the children could share. So why don't you come?"

"That would be wonderful!" I said. "But where will you and your husband sleep?"

"Oh, don't worry about that," she replied. "We have some cots we'll set up in the basement. We do that all the time. Won't you come?"

"Yes! Well, if you're certain. That's great! We will."

I was amazed at her generosity and positive spirit. Imagine that! She was going to make sure that we would have a place to stay, even at the expense of giving up her own bedroom.

It was a glorious, uplifting weekend. The beautiful weather continued. Although the house was not white clapboard, it certainly was a working farmhouse with large barns, many milking cows, and quite a bit of potato acreage. The house, which could have come out of an earlier century, was painted a light brown. Since the family was Mennonite and not Amish, electricity and some appliances (like a washing machine) were evident in the house. And yes, the wash was blowing on the line in the backyard. However, there was no television set.

Although they did not own a car, keeping horses for transportation, Mrs. Olsen told me that they used taxis, trains, planes, and buses on occasion. Her father lived with them and was in charge of the horses and the buggies. Watching him hitching one of the horses up to a black buggy touched my heart, knowing that once my great-grandparents had done the same.

There was more to do than we had anticipated. For example, we all had fun talking to the parrot that lived over the washing machine. Every time Mr. Olsen walked by the parrot would say "Daddy, daddy? Where are you? Come here, Daddy." It would not be satisfied until Mr. Olsen came over and talked to his parrot.

We were also amused, and a bit threatened, by Frankie, the farm's guard dog—except he wasn't a dog. He was a giant goose that could nip you. He protected the cows and made sure nobody went near their fences. Frankie had a great story. Lost and stranded during a hurricane, he had landed in a tree where he got stuck. After the Olsen's freed him, he stayed on their property, never to leave. Gradually, he designed the role of guard for himself. He had piercing blue eyes and a nasty voice. They had named him "Frankie" because his blue eyes were reminiscent of Frank Sinatra's.

Over the weekend, we were able to watch a baby calf. It had been born during the night and was struggling to stand on wobbling legs next to its mother. I was also able to pick potatoes with Mr. Olsen and enjoyed the deep, dark, musty-smelling earth. As a family, we took several long walks through miles and miles of farmland. We had a deep and luxuriant sleep in extremely comfortable beds with wonderful, white Amish quilts pulled over us. Breakfast was a hearty meal, which we enjoyed in the farm's kitchen along with Mrs. Olsen and the other guests.

I had plenty of opportunity to talk with Mrs. Olsen and hear some of her life's story. She was the mother of eight children, all grown now. One son had died of cancer as a young adult. She certainly did not appear bereft. She possessed an excellent sense of humor and a positive view of life, despite the loss of her son. She was busy with grandchildren and visitors from around the world. When I looked through her guest book, as she urged, I realized that she had traveled the world without leaving home. Guests from Japan, Canada, Australia, England, China, and even New Zealand had visited. She talked about many of them, remembering who they were and what they did. Obviously, she relished her friendships with them.

The weekend on the Mennonite farm softened me and opened my soul. By the time we left, my heart was brimming over. I had a sense of the Divine coming through in ordinary life. I craved a way to bring home that sense of the Divine. I didn't realize at that time but it became apparent over the next year that the weekend had fueled courage—my courage to return to Judaism. As beautiful as the weekend was, it still left me with a bit of "soul" pain. I began to realize that this "soul pain" was the result of experiencing the Divine through others' traditions rather than my own! I needed to connect with my own tribe. For years there had been a vacuum in my life around my own traditions. I didn't have a clear sense of what it meant to be a Jewish woman. Now, I was no longer satisfied experiencing that wonderful sense of the Divine via other people's traditions. Why couldn't I experience the Divine through my tradition? After all, I was not a Mennonite, nor would I ever be. Couldn't I feel that closeness to the Divine with my own people?

Over time, I would often think about how the Divine had so beautifully entered the life of Mrs. Olsen. I could clearly see how Mennonite traditions had enhanced her life. She had used the life prescribed by her religion as a guidepost for her own spiritual and emotional growth and for her daily patterns of living. Though she lived on a farm and seldom traveled, she worked within her universe. She was a part of her world and was always true to herself. She turned her farmhouse into a loving guest home. She spent time with her children and grandchildren. And she found her own unique way to travel - by having others come to her. In other words, she'd found a way to meet her own needs while keeping alive the traditions and beliefs of her community.

I thought about her and I asked myself, "What would my life be like—my experiences, my sense of self—if I, too, could be true to myself within the framework of being a Jewish woman?"

A bell went off inside of my head. My life. This was my life and no one else's. I suddenly knew it was time to go back home, to the part of me I had lost long ago. That part of me had been thrown out, like the baby with the bath water. Before I was born, my grandparents had encouraged my parents to remove the Jewish clutter that labeled us and exposed us as Jews in America. "Don't bother to keep kosher; it is an unnecessary nuisance. Don't bother to keep Shabbos—no one does anymore. Don't even look Jewish if you can possibly help it! Get your nose done, if necessary. Put in your contact lenses, stand up straight, and blend in."

And blend in we did.

Now, here I was years later, married and a psychologist, with two nearly grown children and one huge pain in my heart. Something was wrong—really wrong. And I believed it had something to do with the baby that had been thrown out with the bath water. The baby was my essence as a Jewish woman, and I needed that back! I realized that the baby was one of the gaps in my being that was creating a hole in my heart!

Come with me now; share my journey as I go in and out of Jewish places, ideas, and ways. Take some time to let the people I've met, their way of life, and the thoughts they shared gently filter through you. View what lands and keep what sticks. I did. What didn't stick, I let go. I encourage you to do the same. Take some time to ponder and reflect after you read each adventure. I encourage you to use each adventure as stimuli for your journey.

I walked many emotional miles before I found delight. Come with me now; the time is ripe! Let the sharing begin!

THE BEGINNING
Go Find Yourself a Teacher

She was wise, she was loving, she was the source of my soul nourishment—was this really happening?

"If you want to grow and you want to find meaning in living your life as a Jewish woman," my teacher told me, "God will help you, even if the opening within you is at first as small as the eye of a needle."

How had I ended up sitting with this glowing woman whose warm, penetrating, soft brown eyes and calming voice were filling me with hope and supplying me with a sense of solidity about who I was, teaching me the wisdom and knowledge I had yearned for?

To answer that question, we need to go back in time to the year before, to my weekend visit to the Mennonite farm. That visit, as much as it had delighted and moved me, had left me with an ache in my heart, an ache that had persisted long after the weekend was over. That was when I had realized the need to find myself within my own tribe, but I had no clue about where to begin.

For an entire year since then, I had been carrying a newspaper in my briefcase. It was a publication of Chabad, an outreach organization of the Lubavitch Hassidim. From time to time, I'd take the newspaper out and read it—not only the articles, which were soothing and informative, but also the list of telephone numbers to call for more

1

information. Then I'd put the newspaper back in my briefcase and forget about it.

I was in my office rummaging through my papers late one Friday afternoon, and I found that newspaper. Impulsively, I dialed one of the numbers. Was I calling a person, an agency, or an answering machine? I had no idea, but it was one of those moments when I felt the earth trembling about me.

The woman who answered the phone had a warm voice, though she sounded slightly harried. I introduced myself, and she told me that she was Mrs. H, the Chabad rabbi's wife. "My family is getting ready for Shabbos," she explained, as if to excuse the sound of the vacuum I could hear in the distance. "But I'm happy to talk to you."

I told her how I'd been longing to find out more about Judaism and to discover my place within it.

She was immediately comforting, assuring me that she understood the journey I was seeking to begin. She asked me to hold on for a moment; she wanted her husband to speak to me.

"Why is he home so early?" I wondered. I later found out that one hour before Shabbos on a late autumn day is a frantic time of cleaning, tidying, bathing children, and doing a final hour's worth of cooking. I'd probably called at the most incredibly awkward time in their entire week. That day, however, I waited to speak to the Rabbi in blissful ignorance.

Like his wife, the Rabbi was warm, reassuring, and inviting. He talked to me about some activities going on in my county and invited me to a Succos party that he was sponsoring in a week. Encouraging me to come, he wished me a good Shabbos.

The following Wednesday, I sat in my car outside the school where the Succos party was taking place. I needed to be alone, knowing at some intuitive, womanly level that once I went to that party, my life would never be exactly the same. Ten minutes passed, yet as much as I resisted entering, I knew that I had to go in. The pressure to attend came from deep within me.

When I finally went inside, I found a festive, eclectic group: Russian immigrants (this was about ten years ago when many Russian Jews were still coming to this country), and people from different backgrounds and walks of life. Some were from an adjacent town that had a Jewish religious community less than four miles from my home. I hadn't even known that a religious community existed nearby.

We sang and ate delicious food—humus, pita bread, olives, pastries, and other treats. Even the Succah (a structure open to the sky and used during Succos for eating and even sleeping) was beautifully decorated: fruits and vegetables and decorations made by the children hung from the bamboo sticks suspended across the top.

While his seven-year-old daughter sat quietly on his lap, the Rabbi gave a short talk. The next speaker gave his talk in Russian. He was followed in turn by an obviously religious man dressed in a black suit and a black hat. Speaking in Hebrew, this man told about his travels through Africa. Although I didn't fully understand the Hebrew, much less Russian, the vibrant electricity in the air drew me in.

Noticing that the men and women sat separately, I had joined a group of Russian women who were warm and friendly but could only barely speak English. Across from me sat two lovely women, one about my age, who turned out to be B'aal Teshuvah. This word usually connotes someone who has become religious, who practices and observes all the traditions and laws. I define the word much more broadly to include any of us who wander and come back to our tribe to find a way to reconnect and to re-identify, on any level of religiosity.

One of the B'aal Teshuvah was Rachel, a beautiful young woman with radiant brown eyes and a penetrating, upbeat smile. After we talked for a few minutes, she opened her pocketbook, removed a piece of paper, and wrote down her phone number. "Come and visit me some time!" she said with sincerity. I took the scrap of paper, knowing that I would indeed call her.

That night I slept deeply and well. I woke from happy dreams with a heightened sense of well-being. Unfortunately, it was tinged with some anxiety, the tenseness that arises when we know that our lives have been juggled a bit, and that things will never again be exactly the same.

Shortly after the party, I visited Rachel and found her to be as warm and engaging as had been my initial impression. (In fact, she's the absent mother in whose living room, you'll read later, my son and I found a peaceful sanctuary one dreary, winter day, even though no one was around.) During the next year I visited her many times, getting to know her and her six roly-poly, effervescent children. Even our families became friends, and in the course of that year, before they moved away, we shared several holidays with them, including a memorable Chanukah. I'll never forget the beautiful moment Rachel, Jake, and their six children danced in a circle together, all of them delighting in the magic of lighting candles in the darkened room.

Rachel introduced me to Claire, the other B'aal Teshuvah woman who had been at the Purim party. Claire and I then met several times, and she graciously tried to answer my questions. Finally, one day she said to me, "You want help, and I can't help you enough, but I know someone who can. Not too long ago, I was just like you. I'd stumbled into a rich Judaism that was so different from the religion I'd known as a girl that I needed help understanding it. Guidance came to me in the form of a wonderful Torah teacher who teaches only women. If you meet with her, I think you will find some of the guidance that you're looking for."

Pleased, I agreed readily. By this time, I had many emotions, not all of them euphoric. If nothing else, I was just beginning to realize how much effort and time it was going to take to integrate my new insights—what I had seen, felt, and learned—into my old self so that "I" would still emerge as a solid person. I wanted to be able to hold on to all the valuable parts of my old identity while incorporating new aspects. As a psychologist, I knew that the road ahead of me was filled with very hard work, a good deal of anxiety, and some prospective bad moments when I would wish that this transformation had never happened. But I also knew that some wonderful feelings were ahead of me. Look at what I'd already accomplished! I'd created profound changes in my life, finding for myself knowledge and feelings that I needed and to which I was genuinely entitled.

Claire introduced me to Leah, who turned out to be exactly the spiritual counselor for whom I'd been hoping and searching. Much of what she helped me work through and understand during those first years of counseling I've written about in my first book, "THE ENCHANTED SELF, A POSITIVE THERAPY". In some ways, Leah helped me to redefine myself as a full, wondrous woman who could take her place in the Jewish tradition proudly—defined in terms of my strengths rather than by the societal distortions lodged deeply in western civilization. How welcome this was! Growing up, I'd always felt so out of place, so out of the loop in a competitive society geared to male superiority. Here, however, I recognized and embraced my role as a female, a focal point of Jewish society.

Leah also gave me the gift of the Torah (first five books of Moses). I was able for the first time to read parts of the first five books of Moses and not feel frustrated and alienated by long lists of names and descendants. Instead, I felt incredibly inspired by the implications inherent in virtually every word in every line. A discussion around any topic—why Joseph's brothers tossed him into the pit, for example, resonated within me endlessly. Such talks gave me the opportunity to think about some of my own deficits, about how often I forget about certain people or diminish them, and about how other people occasionally put me aside.

With Leah's help, for the first time in my life I was able to prepare for Passover. I cooked and cleaned and felt ready for the holiday in a way I never had. It took my husband and me a while, but eventually we realized that we'd been lighting candles and enjoying a Shabbos dinner each Friday night without even realizing it—that we were not going to the movies or the mall, or meeting friends at a Chinese restaurant, but spending time together at home or with friends who also valued the quiet beauty of Shabbos.

My life was changing, and Leah was my guide. This was about the time that I began to take notes on significant moments in my Judaic journey. I was motivated to do this partly because I was so amazed and surprised at my new feelings that I needed to write about them so that I could relive the magic again and again. However, I also felt that I needed to document certain aspects of Judaism as I discovered them to reinforce my learning.

I saw the magic of what I was learning and experiencing in my enchanted Judaic journey as not only necessary knowledge for me, but as knowledge that should be shared, wisdom for all to learn. Every insight dovetailed one hundred percent with the psychological concepts that I was developing in The Enchanted Self, which is based on the concept that we can all enjoy positive states of well-being and live lives of meaning and positive action if we take the time to educate ourselves in these processes. We all need to learn to practice positive habits. It's an essential teaching, and one that unfortunately our society largely ignores.

In retrospect, that first year of my introduction to Judaism was the hardest but also the most beautiful year of my adult life. It was hard because every new bit of knowledge about my tribe, about the wisdom and laws that composed the core components of Jewish practices, had a ripple effect, not only on my own emotions and spiritual life,

8

but on those of my family as well. My whole worldview—and theirs—became changed forever.

The stories that I'm sharing with you are the result of ten years of journaling. Like fine grains of sand that were once jumbled and chaotic, these stories have sifted through the hourglass of time and now lie still on the bottom of the glass. There may be more disruptions ahead in my life, as there will be in all of our lives, for the hourglass never stays put; it gets turned over again and again. For right now, however, let's delight and share in the purity of those quiescent grains of sand and just enjoy the moments I offer to you in the following pages.

Ponderings

Have you ever felt the earth tremble around you, knowing that from this moment forward your life would shift forever?

You may want to reflect on those times, remembering what changes occurred as a consequence. Just sit back and enjoy the memories and feelings related to the fabric of your life!

LOAVES OF LOVE
My Tribe Welcomes Me Back!

It was a Wednesday morning and the air was soft and warm. Mid-April is a luscious time of year, when feelings of hope bubble up inside of me once again, when I feel uplifted and capable of growth, change, and adventure. But I was a little uneasy this morning because I had planned a very unusual day for myself. First I would be driving into the heart of Borough Park via Staten Island. My first challenge would be to avoid unpleasant feelings as I navigated the car over two bridges. I've never enjoyed driving on high bridges. Some of my worst nightmares have been about being on bridges that either gave way or suddenly had parts missing.

However I would gladly meet that challenge today because I was going to spend time with Miriam, a new friend. We had met through my cousin and had instantly taken to each other, although our worlds are very, very different. She had grown up in an orthodox Jewish home and has always been religious. I had grown up knowing that I was Jewish, but I had often been caught in the emotional strain of my parents' unresolved feelings about being Jewish. She'd studied in a religious girl's high school, while I went to public high school, actually in the town where my dad was one of the first Jewish superintendent's of public schools in the country. She had married, had six children, and lived in the heart of Borough Park. I had gone to a prestigious, secular, girl's college, married, had two children and lived in a suburb.

Yet Miriam and I always had a great time together, chatting, sharing, and learning from one another. Today, when I arrived at her house, she'd put out a lovely platter of nuts and dried fruits, and she was serving me cookies and fresh coffee before I could say "No." Yes, my trip had been slightly fatiguing, but I was being treated much more royally than I had expected.

After a good deal of noshing and catching up with each other, we were ready for the special treat of the day-driving to the home of Toby, "the challah lady", where we'd have a joint challah-baking lesson. I was surprised that Miriam didn't know how to bake challah, since she cooked everything else for her large family. She explained that it had always seemed so time-consuming, and although she could bake challah, she wanted a lesson to really refine her capacities, particularly braiding the dough, which was difficult. Now that she had a little more time, with several of her children already married and out of the house, she was ready to put the time into the weekly baking.

The street was busy—cars, mothers and baby carriages, children hanging at their mother's sides, bookstores, food stores, clothing stores, shoe stores—a potpourri of life and business. All the men were dressed in black outfits of one combination or another. Some had long sidelocks, some had short; some had on what almost looked like knickers while others wore very conservative but standard black trousers. The women all wore dresses or suits and raincoats and covered their hair with "shaitels" (wigs). Some even wore hats on top of their wigs. The neighborhood seemed wholesome, but I felt like a stranger. I was wearing what the other women wore—long skirt, raincoat, and hat—but sharing an outfit couldn't bridge the gap that resulted from living in very different worlds for so many years.

Toby's world was even further from mine than Miriam's. Coming to greet us at the door, a comfortable housecoat zipped over her body and a kerchief tied around her head, Toby welcomed us. Her home was remarkably simple. It looked like a cold-water flat with a few small rooms, bare wood floor, walls with no pictures, the basic, simple furnishings, and a kitchen out of the 1940s with no major appliances; but immediately I was comfortable in it. Pleasant Jewish music wafted in from outside, along with children's laughter, household sounds, and muffled car noises. It was much more pleasing than the blaring sounds of a television.

Toby was quite obviously pregnant but did not speak of it, nor did we. A three-year-old boy clung to her apron strings, but the rest of the household, composed of about ten children ranging in age from toddlers to young adults, were not in evidence—they were apparently either in school or married. I couldn't imagine how Toby lived with all those children and yet had such radiance about her. Her skin was smooth and fresh, and her big smile was warm and engaging.

How did she have the time to do her nearly daily "mitzvah" (good deed, connecting in positive ways) of teaching women to bake challah? What was pushing her to do it? When I asked her, she told us that she did it because it was such a great mitzvah to bake challah. She explained that God had given Jewish women the honor of blessing the challah. It was her pleasure to teach us, the many of us who didn't know that.

Joy poured out of her as she showed us how to save a piece of dough and "make a blessing" on it. Her energy affected me so much, I felt connected to women of the desert, ancestors I would never know. I could almost feel the pulse and see the hands of thousands of years of women at work kneading dough, as Toby talked about how this practice went back to the days of the ancient temples.

Toby's kitchen was old-fashioned but perfectly clean—with not even a crumb in sight. She asked us whether we'd rather roll out the dough by hand or use the machine she had. Both Miriam and I indicated that we preferred to roll out the dough by hand, Toby seemed delighted with our decision. She watched with pride as we kneaded the dough.

What a transforming experience this was! I felt as if God's feminine side was whispering in my ear, "You have a wonderful task to do and it involves working this dough to the point of pure pleasure."

For half an hour I pressed, rolled, pushed, pulled, squeezed, turned, and lifted the dough as vigorously as I could. Toby, an instinctively good teacher, praised my kneading technique and the strength of my hands. I found myself talking about my grandmother and the challah she had made when I was young. My hands, it seemed, had been inherited from a long line of women empowered by a sacred undertaking.

Miriam, who was also working hard, beamed as she kneaded the dough. When our hands and arms grew tired, Toby encouraged us to rest and have a snack. We nibbled on delicious marble cake, creamy cheesecake, and homemade coffee ice cream, all handmade from the egg whites left over from challah baking.

After our snack, we returned to our baking. Toby produced a bowl in which the challah had already risen. That's when I realized that the batch I had fashioned would be presented to Toby's next student—a woman I didn't know but to whom I was giving something very special, just as strangers had bequeathed this kneading challah to me.

I cut my new dough into six pieces, each of which I then rolled into long, thin strips. Toby showed me how to braid them. I tried to follow her as she spoke. "Bring these two strips close together and then bring this one under them. Then it goes up over the right (or did she say left?). Then the other goes down, and then you start all over." I loved braiding the dough.

After all the loaves were shaped, we made some miniature loaves with the leftover dough. Then everything went into the oven. Toby invited us to shop in the neighborhood while the bread baked, and we did. Miriam knew all the best places to frequent—a great shoe store, a hat boutique, and finally a Jewish bookstore filled with a seemingly endless supply of books. The time flew.

As we returned, Toby was walking down the steps from her house with big gray plastic garbage bags in her hands, bags filled with the fruit of our labor. She placed the bags in the passenger and back seats of my car. We hugged and kissed each other. She told us to come back any time for another lesson.

I dropped Miriam and her challah at her house and then headed for New Jersey. I imagined Toby climbing the steps back to her family as I headed toward the Staten Island bridges.

It was rush hour, but I was calm. I felt as if I had accomplished something special, a feeling I hadn't had for years, perhaps not since I was a girl and learned how to skip or ride my bike. The aroma of bread filled the car and the memory of making it replenished me. I had enough challah to last a month, and I enjoyed the restorative sense of a job well done.

It was still light when I got home, even after I put the challahs in the freezer. I took my tape recorder and walked around the block. I had begun keeping a personal journal of my Judaic, spiritual adventures, and I wanted to capture this one while it was as fresh as my newly baked challah. I was still in a heightened state of pleasure. The entire day had energized me and aroused joyous feelings. I wanted to share the day, but I didn't know exactly with whom at that point. So I talked to myself on my tape recorder and went over my afternoon many times in my mind.

A year or two later, I heard a woman speak at New York City's Carlbach Synagogue about the heightened experiences she had while making challah. This speaker lived in the mountains outside Denver, Colorado. She shared how fervently she waited for Thursdays, challah preparation night, and how she stayed up by herself, into the wee hours, lovingly baking her challahs. She, like Toby, had an intense reaction to the special prayer said when kneading the challah. She so lovingly described her time making bread that I pictured her in a kitchen on the frontier, the darkness illuminated only by the stars in the sky and the glow in her as she made the special bread. She stirred up a desire within me to also invest that type of energy and passion in such a beautiful act.

Would I give the time? Could I give the time? The one lesson from Toby would obviously never be enough. I would need more lessons. Additionally, the hour or two that I might set aside to do some home cooking and preparations for Shabbat certainly would not be enough. This required a commitment beyond a scant 60 or 90 minutes a week.

I realized with a small shock that my world had begun to shift. Women from my family, those long dead women who would have loved me if they had known me, women who had prayed for me knowing that I would someday exist—as well as my living female relatives and women like Miriam and Toby who had reached out to me—all these women became beacons beckoning to me, joined in a circle as sisters. I felt all their strong hands and could see them all kneading the challah dough on breadboards along with me. Unrushed, we shared conversation and good food. No one expected me to know more than I did; there appeared to be no limit to the age at which one could learn a new skill. It was never too late. I relaxed in the shared sacred time of women of the past and present.

The door was open. My tribe was welcoming me back home. This powerful experience was truly an Enchanted Self experience.

The day had provided me with many keys to a meaningful life experience. Miriam's and Toby's sincere warmth and genuine caring had richly augmented my sense of liking myself, and I felt I knew more about who I am. The day had provided me with tribal information and a sense of belonging to a long line of special women. I felt that I had acquired a new skill, at least in part, and my emotional, spiritual needs had been fully met for the moment. I had help in learning from Toby, my mentor. I had experienced a sense of pleasure and had ended the day in a euphoric state. Furthermore, I had shared in the world of good deeds and positive action.

Not only would this day long stay with me, but it inspired me to seek many chances to transmit the essence of this day to other people, particularly women. I hoped to be able to use my day as an example of how we can help each other experience so much well-being that we each have a chance for enchantment.

Reflections

You may want to reflect on those times in your life where you had a full, rich experience that led to happiness and a feeling that you were thriving. If you've had such an occasion, permit yourself time to reminisce so that you can enjoy the occasion again and again. Share. Tell your children. It's worth it. You can really light up someone else's life just by sharing your moment of enchantment.

You may also want to think about creating a day full of good intentions and fervent dedication to yourself or to others you care about. Take the time to brainstorm what you might be able to offer someone that would be the kind of gift that Toby gave to me. Or maybe you'd rather dream about what you wish someone would want to offer you. Enjoy dreaming, imagining, or planning.

MUSINGS
Meeting Our Needs

We all have needs, it's only natural, but having needs can cause us pain. I discovered this both in the treatment room with my clients and in my own life. Of course, there are different levels of needs, corresponding to different intensities of pain.

Even though we're grown-up chronologically, many of us find that the skills we need to live emotionally satisfying lives are underdeveloped. Many of my clients need help, for instance, in learning to negotiate the garden-variety aggravations in their lives.

I help my clients address what they need by teaching them how to speak up in appropriate ways to their husbands, to be firm yet loving with their children, to approach a boss with a complaint or a request for a raise, to mend fences with a parent or a sibling. Once we learn these skills, we feel more in command of our lives, and therefore more adequate. We feel that we're heard, and that makes us feel proud.

However, other needs run even deeper than the need to be heard and to feel competent. If unaddressed, these needs result in something that I call "soul pain," because so many people have described it to me by saying, "I feel as if I have an ache in my soul." Relieving this pain requires true self-knowledge. In my treatment room, I help clients deal with their soul pain by helping each to discover her Enchanted Self.

"Who are you?" I ask my clients. "What is the essence of your sense of self, your purpose?"

I call this process of gaining self-knowledge "learning the song of your soul." Once you have a profound knowledge about who you really are—know what you value and what's relevant to your life—you're in a better position to meet your deep needs.

For example, one of my clients had struggled for years to identify her true interest—she didn't know if she was primarily an artist or a scientist. She was finally able to acknowledge and understand that she didn't have to choose between her interests, that she was both an artisan and a scientist. That discovery enabled her to restructure her life. She found a job in a laboratory and relaxed in the evenings in a ceramics studio, designing and creating beautiful pottery.

My own soul pain wasn't about my work but about my spiritual needs. Eventually, I found a way to address my needs by returning to my tribe. To me, discovering Judaism was like meeting a beautiful woman wrapped in seven veils. As she shed each veil, my heart yearned to come closer to her, to touch her, to be part of her, and to learn what lies beneath the next veil.

Many of the stories I write recount the moment a veil is lifted and I moved a little bit closer to the mystery commanding my attention.

Our soul needs are uniquely ours. Yet I share my stories with you regardless, because I know that women need to listen to each other's soul hungers and because by sharing we nurture each other.

MY TRIPS TO THE MIKVAH
It's Never Too Late!

It was autumn again, and the Jewish High Holy Days were upon us. This year I was to have a new experience: I was going to go to the Mikvah. A moving body of pure water, the Mikvah has various sacred purposes that have been passed down for thousands of years. This was my first visit and I was excited and scared; still, I wouldn't have missed this opportunity.

Going to the Mikvah was a special treat, even though I had found out about this ritual late in life—too late to consider using it on a regular monthly basis. I'd heard other women talk about it, but it had always seemed very archaic, something that women used before good home plumbing was widely available. My mother never went there, nor had her mom. My dad's mother had used the Mikvah only when she was in Poland.

When I was newly married, we lived on Washington Street in Brighton, Massachusetts, in an apartment building exactly three doors away from Boston's Mikvah. I walked past it at least five times a week, going to and from the trolley on Commonwealth Avenue. I would look at the wooden clapboard siding and think nothing of it; it was simply not part of my life. In those years, I was in conflict with being Jewish. Much of my heritage seemed anachronistic and meaningless.

I had never thought about the Mikvah until recently, when I was reading a pamphlet on the origins and the beauty of the Mikvah experience, called "The Purifying Waters". I cried for two hours. Ironically those tears, my own water drops pouring out of me, were the final acknowledgment that I had missed the gift of the purifying waters, a gift of my own heritage. I mourned that the Mikvah couldn't be part of my life—not because I didn't want it to, but because I was now middle-aged. The days when I might have observed the Laws of Purity on a monthly basis had passed for me. This made me sad and angry. Simply stated, the laws are that you don't have marital relations during your menstruation or for a week afterwards. Then you go to the Mikvah, and afterwards, you resume relations with your husband until the next cycle.

The anger finally began to subside, and it was replaced with a gift! Actually, God presented me with two gifts. One I used only once, and the other many times. Let me tell you about the first.

A dear friend and mentor explained to me that even an older woman may go to the Mikvah once to celebrate her marriage. She encouraged me to do so, to go as a "bride", convincing me that I was entitled to the experience. Twenty-eight years after my wedding, I drove to the Mikvah in Lakewood, as my friend had arranged.

The sun was setting, the sky streaked in various shades of pink. By the time I parked the car, it was deep, dark twilight. A warm and efficient middle-aged woman ushered me into the "bridal" chamber. I was euphoric. She explained the procedure and left me to luxuriate in a warm bath, where I was charged to cleanse my toenails and fingernails, take out my contact lenses, and otherwise prepare myself.

After a short time, she knocked and entered. Curiosity got the best of me. I discovered that she was the mother of eight grown children. She had worked at the Mikvah for years and really enjoyed her work. I didn't ask her age, but assumed that she was about five years younger than I. I had a fleeting fantasy—what would my life have been like if I had been a Mikvah matron instead of a psychologist? I had a feeling that the work was delicate and involved giving advice and sharing secrets, just like my work.

The matron took me down to the Mikvah and guided me through a prayer that I was to recite. The water was warm and comforting. She watched to make sure that I fully immersed myself three times after the prayer. I then returned to my changing room, took a quick shower and left. And there was my friend, waiting for me, with a present of scented soaps. How sensitive and womanly! The whole experience filled me with an inner glow, a feeling of anticipation, as if I were a much younger woman about to have a special first night with her husband.

Driving home from Lakewood, I really looked forward to seeing my husband and to our time together, such was the power behind the Mikvah experience. I thought about all the women I'd read about and heard of who walked in snow to get to the Mikvah to honor the Laws of Purity. I now understand why.

This bridal ritual was a one-time only occasion. I regretted that. I knew through many years of living that experiences become richer, fuller, and more layered if we repeat them. However, once was better than nothing.

Only later did I learn that I could attend the Mikvah at least twice a year, on the mornings before Rosh Hashanah (The Jewish New Year) and Yom Kippur (The Day of Atonement.) In a near-by Sephardic community the Mikvah was open to Jewish women for the purpose of personal sacred prayer. This was a new beginning! This time, though, I would not be monitored; I would be alone in the Mikvah for as long as I wanted to be, I could talk to God, and I could choose when to dunk myself.

I parked my car and walked into a beautiful foyer with comfortable chairs, a mahogany desk, lovely pictures of flowers blanketing the walls, and marble flooring. It was very modern and elegant—and best of all, no one was there! I was totally alone. I enjoyed the sense of privacy all the more because the peaceful silence of the water as it flowed around me somehow conveyed the feeling that I was part of a long line of women enjoying this cleansing tradition, a line that stretched far into the past, and that will doubtless flow long into the future.

A sign on the desk asked for a donation of twenty dollars, if possible. I appreciated the great sense of trust that the sign reflected. I also loved knowing what to do and where to go.

I walked down a corridor and opened a door, finding a dressing room that seemed clean and luxurious despite the few towels on the floor. I closed both doors, which were fully lined with mirrors, and proceeded to undress, take out my contact lenses, and prepare for the Mikvah. I immediately felt immersed in a special environment that brought back vague yet somehow powerful awareness of being female. These feelings of belonging to a group, a clan, were such positive feelings. I felt such love for "us"—all of us who had come and gone, had children, laughed, been beautiful, cried, prayed, grown old, and loved.

I felt good inside. This was a positive connection, one not tied to gossip, put-downs, criticisms, or comparisons. I felt a connection to others that wasn't based on age or body; it was as if all the women I knew had been branded with a primitive imprint that identified us as belonging to the same clan. On this level of awareness there were no words, just timeless knowledge—knowledge of mannerisms and hopes and dreams that transcended time. Joined together, we all enjoyed the prerogative to go through this ritual together, even though we each did it separately. I was so moved that I cried as I stepped out of my clothes.

After changing, I went down the hall to the Mikvah. I walked down the staircase and immersed myself to chest level in the warm, very pleasant water. As soon as my arms were on top of the water, resting gently, I had another elevated sense of connection. This was different from the sense of being one with all the females of my tribe—this was a feeling of a holy connection to God. I even felt a connection to the great Divine, to the messengers, angels, and caring beings seeming to hover around me. I was not scared; in fact, I had a profound feeling of being protected and loved. I found myself in so much awe that I couldn't remember the prayers I had so carefully composed the night before.

It didn't matter. I prayed anyway. The words tumbled out of me until I was done. Then I immersed myself totally in the Mikvah. After the initial shock of immersion subsided, I climbed out and walked back down the hall. I showered and dressed, feeling content. This was a private time, a gentle time. It was a time when a woman could finally take her time preparing herself, growing whole. Yet it was different from the time you spend nervously fixing yourself up before a party, primping in front of the mirror, trying to look beautiful. This was a time of integration and of moving from the spiritual to the physical. It was a time of supreme peace and beauty.

This Mikvah experience heightened Yom Kippur for me that year. I had been given two gifts: a one-time experience in Lakewood and another that will continue for many years. These two gifts took away my tears and replaced them with pleasure, a spiritual high, and a connection to the wonderful tribal world of Jewish women. I felt as if my cries had been heard and answered.

It's never too late! We never know when we'll be presented with the opportunity to reinvent ourselves—an opportunity that we didn't even know existed. I know; it happened to me!

Ponder and Muse

Has your world ever suddenly opened up and a new door appeared? Perhaps, a door you had given up hope of opening or would never have dreamed existed?

On the other hand, would you like a chance to come around again to something special? Think about opening your heart and giving the universe permission to find ways to bring something special back around to you. This may take time and may require some reinvention on your part, but it is worth it!

LOCKS OF LOVE
A Special Treat for a Little Boy and for Me!

It was a cold, rainy, gray wintry day. The local Chabad Rabbi had invited me to attend his young son's Upsherin, which means "haircutting ceremony." Though I didn't know what to expect, I was in for a bit of an adventure on this otherwise miserable day.

I had vague memories of my dad telling me that his hair had not been cut until he was three. He'd had blonde ringlets, and everyone stopped his mother on the street to say how beautiful his hair was. This was a sweet and interesting story, but it bore no connection to my life. It was as remote as the photograph of him, at age seven, sitting on a spotted pony in front of his house in New Haven, Connecticut. The fact that people still housed horses in small barns on their property when my dad was a boy and that, as a young teenager, he'd driven a horse and wagon making deliveries around the neighborhood was nothing but a curiosity to me. After all, my father and I loved each other, but we existed in different worlds, or thus it often seemed.

That cold, rainy Sunday, I found myself standing in line with many other friends and relatives of the Rabbi and Rebbetzein in the reception hall of our local religious school. The boy had at least nine or ten siblings, and all were there as well. What was I doing in this long line?

The Rabbi explained that each of us would get a chance to cut a tiny bit of hair from the boy's locks as we walked by him. At first I thought the little boy would be frightened and crying, but I quickly saw that this was not the case. There he was, standing on top of a table and draped in his father's "Tallis," or prayer shawl (which for him was like a giant king's cloak), looking as happy as a three-year-old could possibly look. I would say he looked radiant. As people walked by snipping off little locks of hair, his parents fed him cookies and candy, hugged him, and told him how great he was doing. He was clearly king for the day—a happy king.

Everyone had a turn with the scissors. That his haircutting was, indeed, a communal event was shocking to me in and of itself. It couldn't have been more foreign to me. My girlhood memories of getting my hair cut were unpleasant, particularly the time when my bangs were cut too short and for several weeks I felt I had been cheated out of my own hair. I very much doubted that this little boy would feel cheated by his experience, surrounded as he was by so much love. In fact, it seemed as if he was being given a message—that he was loved and special—which was reinforced every moment. He didn't have to be more than he was, a three-year-old boy. His job was only to stand there, eat cookies, and be loved. And he did it well!

After the haircutting ceremony was over, someone who seemed to know how to cut hair finished shaping up the boy's locks. Then, the rabbi encouraged us to follow as he took the boy into a classroom and lovingly showed him the "Aleph Beth", or the ABCs of Hebrew letters. The youngster put his finger on different letters, and his father would say the name. Clearly, he was being introduced to the concept of formal schooling, which would now begin for him. I couldn't help but think of what a wonderful experience he'd have in school from this day forward, thanks to being surrounded by so much love on the day of his initiation.

The day ended with more delights—all of the guests were ushered back into the big reception room, where we enjoyed a lovely feast of delicacies and sweets.

By the time I had left the school, the sky had cleared and I was filled with wonder over the ritual I'd witnessed. I was impressed with the special treatment bestowed on this boy, and how he was encouraged to feel not only special but also happy and joyful as he started his schooling. He had looked so adorable wrapped up in his father's prayer shawl. He must have known how special it was to wear this extraordinary garment, and that it reflected his father's high esteem for him. What wonderful feelings he had taken inside of himself—and these would all help him to build his own sense of self. He was being given a present, a very special present. But it wasn't from "Toys 'R Us". Instead, it came from the very heart of Jewish tradition. It was a present that went back thousands of years. It was a present given in the hope that the boy would go on to have an education in the Torah, the sacred books of Judaism, and would one day pass his knowledge on to the next generation.

A few years later, I went to see the movie, "A World Apart". Again I had the pleasure of watching as a young boy had his first haircut. Though it took place at home rather than a reception hall, many of the other details were similar. However one scene was strikingly different. After the ceremony, as the boy was being taken from his home to a "Cheder" (Jewish religious school) down the block, where he would begin learning the Aleph Beth, he was wrapped in the Tallis so that it entirely covered his body and his face. Of course it was a loose shawl so he could easily breathe.

The movie went on to explain that the boy's grandfather had wrapped him in the shawl so thoroughly because the boy was in a state of purity, and the older man didn't want anything outside contaminating his grandson on his brief journey. Obviously, his grandfather couldn't protect him forever, but this was a special day, and every effort at protection had to be made.

This scene moved me tremendously. It pulled from my memory my father's story about his own golden locks. My dad had become a great educator but also had remained a life-long student, someone who always loved to learn. Was his career choice influenced by his special day? I saw now that we were part of a different place. We came from different times. I also realized that, sadly, we were of different traditions, my father and I—and it was my loss. I had fallen out of my own tradition, the tradition in which he was raised, and now I wanted nothing more than to return at least to the essence, if not the actual tradition.

Muse and Ponder

Have you ever heard about something that seemed irrelevant to you, not of importance to your own time or place, only to discover later on that it was indeed very important? Jot down whatever memories come to mind.

Is there anything that you have heard about in your family tradition that you might be curious to explore? If so, maybe now is the time to find out a little more about it.

Discovering family traditions connects you to your people in a special way. It also enables you to pass on the tradition to the next generation.

Sometimes, you discover a tradition only to realize that you're too late for it. I, for instance, discovered the haircutting ritual when my son was grown. He would never have the opportunity to undergo the Upsherin.

Fortunately, there are always new rituals you can create. You can decide to bake special cookies with your grandchildren for the holidays. You can decide to treat all the younger members of your family to a special day at the theater on their sixteenth birthdays. You might even go on a special summer camping trip with those family members who are leaving for college in the fall.

I hope you will find ways to bring life-enhancing, self-esteem-boosting rituals into your world.

A WINDOW BEGINS TO OPEN...
"Holy Days", by Liz Harris,
Becomes a Book of Enlightenment for Me!

Someone—I can't remember whom—suggested that I read the book Holy Days by Liz Harris. That happens so often in our lives: we're given something that seems unremarkable only to realize later that it was a precious gift, something we needed at that very moment, as vital as the final piece of an unfinished jigsaw puzzle. Only by the time we realize it, the person who gave it to us is gone, without our having had the chance to say, "Thank you."

I'd never heard of the book, but I was able to order it. From the first page, I found myself mesmerized. Ms. Harris, a journalist for "The New York Times", had decided to spend time with a group of Hassidic families from the Lubavitch sect, who live in Williamsburg, Brooklyn. The book is an account of her observations and what she learned.

The book was quite a revelation; it shifted my view of the world forever. Since I knew virtually nothing of the history of the Hassidic movement, I was surprised to learn that its founder, the B'aal Shem Tov, was a nineteenth-century rabbi in Eastern Europe who taught his followers to cultivate their capacity for joy. In terms of Judaism, this is a relatively recent movement.

But Ms. Harris does much more than merely provide a history of the movement. She also charts her own reactions to the community, which parallel mine. Raised in the Conservative movement, she felt as if she were a spectator watching a game she had never been invited to play. That's pretty much how I felt, except I didn't even know what sport I was watching! My early experiences with Judaism left me feeling empty, as if I'd been expecting to go to a ball game or circus, but instead of going into the facility, I was left outside on a park bench.

I'd never known that Judaism could be so infused with ecstasy and joyfulness. To learn about this whole other aspect of my own religion was like opening a door in my house that had been closed my whole life.

I grew up "almost Gentile" in Norwalk, Connecticut, where learning about my religion meant trying to memorize the Hebrew alphabet but failing, as my learning disabilities were never acknowledged or understood. In Norwalk, Jewish Talmudic thought (methods of thinking used to interpret the Torah) might be deciding whether keeping kosher meant you could order a bacon, lettuce, and tomato sandwich at the local diner but not have it at home.

My family and I had attended sterile High Holy Day Jewish services held in a large public assembly hall owned by the city, because there was no reform synagogue sanctuary large enough to hold all of us who were "High Holy Day Jews". Going to temple was like receiving a remnant of cloth—I could tell it had once been beautiful, but by the time it was handed to me, the piece of cloth seemed tattered, small, and inconsequential.

Organ music filled the building, reminding me more of church than a synagogue. I was given a reform prayer book that, at the time, imitated the look of a Christian prayer book. And as for passion, the only question in which I was passionately interested was exactly how long it would take the rabbi to finish the responsive reading and move through the rest of the pages until we reached the red ribbon marking the end of the morning's service. Then finally, <u>finally</u>, we could go home.

I could never have articulated my feelings then, but I knew something was very wrong. I'm not making a judgment on Reform Judaism, or on any form of Judaism for that matter. All the different movements evolved over time for very specific reasons. I'm not in a position to compare them. All I know is that for me, Reform Judaism didn't work.

For years I felt I was alone with these thoughts. Reading Liz Harris, I realized that I wasn't alone. Her feelings about her lost connection to Judaism validated mine. Maybe I wasn't a freak after all; maybe my hunger for more—even though I couldn't have articulated what "more" meant—wasn't a problem at all but a wholesome, good thing.

As I continued to read the book, I began to have a sense of what "more" meant to me. In one section, Harris recounts spending Purim with a woman named Sheina and her family. The day Harris arrived, Sheina was busy making packages of Shalach Manot, which are baskets that filled with hamentaschen (triangular, filled pastry), grape juice, nuts, and chocolate and are distributed to friends, neighbors, and children. Later, the children would dress up in colorful costumes and go to the synagogue, where they listen to the reading of the Megillah, the story of how Queen Esther saved the Jews from annihilation. What a festive, busy holiday!

Purim had come and gone many times over my lifetime, but it was a holiday that had barely existed for me. As a child I'd delivered hamentaschen when I belonged to a youth group. When I had children of my own, I'd taken them to one or two Purim festivals sponsored by our local synagogue. Other than that, the holiday had escaped my notice. I never noted it on my calendar and never changed my schedule because of it.

However, as I read about Sheina and her family and how they celebrated Purim, I felt an incredible hunger arise inside me, a hunger for the vitality that was in this woman's life—not only on Purim but every day. I even cried in acknowledgment of my regret. I was in real pain.

At the time I had no idea how I could move toward reincorporating the holiday into my life. I hope that by sharing my reactions to Liz Harris' book with you, you'll know how much of a true miracle my Purim story, "Thank You, Mr. Moon", really is.

THANK YOU, MR. MOON
AND THANK YOU, MR. AND MRS. HABERMAN
Purim - A Day of Miracles

You know how sometimes, when you look up at the moon, you really do see the exquisitely carved face of the man in the moon, his smile, his chiseled nose, and his penetrating eyes? His stark beauty always comforts me. I believe that God imprinted that face on the moon so that each of us will always know that our earth is God's special home for us.

One night last March, I looked up at the moon, as full as it could be, and realized that Mr. Man in the Moon was smiling down right at me. His warmth reached me through all the millions of miles, reinforcing the warmth of my full day. My belly full after eating a festive meal and my mood happy, I winked at him, and he winked right back. I felt as if we were co-conspirators in pleasure, secretly acknowledging the unusually raucous festive day I had just celebrated.

I was returning home after spending the Jewish holiday of Purim in Monsey, a religious community near New York City. Purim is a marvelous holiday dedicated to acknowledging God's hidden powers. It is celebrated on the fourteenth day of Adar, usually in our month of March, and marks the day the Jews in the Persian Empire rested from their miraculous victory over the forces threatening to overcome them.

Back in 357 BCE, evil Persian King Achashverous agreed to let his evil henchman, Haman, lead a murderous attack on the Jews who lived in Persia. Queen Esther, Achashverous' Hebrew wife, took courageous steps that led to a series of hidden miracles resulting in Haman's defeat and death and the lifting of the edict to kill all the Jews. Queen Esther then ordered that the events be recorded in what is known as "Megillas Esther." It is a powerful story of good overcoming evil, and it may well be one of the first documents ordered by a woman to be recorded by scribes.

Many people don't understand the nature of Purim. I didn't. I thought of it as a silly holiday, mostly for children. When my children were young, I dressed them up, took them to Purim carnivals, and watched them play games. I was always eager for the festivities to be over so that we could go home.

However, attending a Purim celebration—a festive meal called a "Seudah"— with my daughter and baby grandson at the Monsey home of Rabbi Haberman and his wife Rachel forever changed the way I thought of the holiday.

Earlier in the evening, as we had approached the house we had heard voices and recorded music pouring out the windows. Welcomed with hugs and kisses from our hostess, we had been led into a small dining room already packed with men, women, children, and babies. I couldn't imagine finding room for two more chairs and a highchair. Little did I know that Purim is a day of miracles.

Once we were settled in, I began to look around me. Many people, not just children, were dressed in colorful costumes. Purim is the holiday when Jews are encouraged to take on a new persona and play at being someone else. Many choose to dress up as Queen Esther and other people from the actual Biblical story, but you are free to be anyone you choose. I was surrounded by girls dressed as brides and boys dressed as policemen and soldiers. Observant teenagers, who normally wear traditional white shirts, black pants, yarmulkes, and payos (long sideburns), appeared incongruous dressing in the secular uniform of typical city teens (baggy pants and oversized tee shirts), carrying gigantic boom boxes, and chanting rap lyrics.

My daughter and I weren't in costume, and neither were many of the men, who wore the black hats and long coats that they always did. But even they stepped out of character, for they were all drinking. They would talk seriously together for a few moments, only to erupt in celebration, stomping their feet, banging their fists on the table, and singing heartily in unison. They were so spirited that the dining room itself began to shake and tremble.

I realized that I felt somewhat overwhelmed in Rachel's dining room. The noisy singing, the raucous tapes of Jewish music playing in the background, the banter, the loud laughter, and the stomping were all strange to me. As welcoming as everyone was, I almost felt as if I were in a new world, far from home. All the women wore shaitels (wigs), and were surrounded by their many children. Their husbands were perpetual students who worked only to make a living, divesting themselves of as many daily chores as possible in order to devote themselves solely to the study of the Torah. Their very private lives were hard for me to imagine. My own family was small and very public, thanks to my work and writing. And my husband had quit Hebrew school as soon as he had been permitted to. Yes, I came from a world very different from theirs.

But when I closed my eyes, my feelings of alienation began to fade and I slowly felt more and more at home. I listened to the men's voices and felt the pulse of their feet beating on the floor. The rhythmic energy began to sound like the churning of a locomotive careening down the track, and it wasn't hard to fantasize that we were all on a train together. It seemed impossible that we were simply sitting in a room. The magnitude of the energy swept us away, hurtling us through space!

At one point, Rabbi Haberman gave a short talk about the holiness of Purim. "Some people consider Purim as sacred a day as Yom Kippur," he said, pointing out that the word "pur", common to both holidays, means to cast your lot. "On Purim", he continued, "the doors are wide open for opening your heart to God and returning to Him in prayer, just as on Yom Kippur." He explained that some people feel that we are even judged on Purim. To me, this meant that I had a chance to work out something spiritual inside me. It was an opportunity for me to pray with all my heart to God.

Purim also resembles, in spirit, another Jewish holiday, Simchat Torah, the day the cycle of reading from the Torah is completed and begun anew. Both holidays encourage jubilant celebration.

Only recently have I come to realize how wise it is to have holidays during which people can really let loose in safe, yet controlled, environments, when it is really okay to get tipsy and silly. To place this kind of celebration entirely off limits wouldn't be healthy—people would find an excuse to act out, since it's hard to be serious all the time. This way, the celebration is contained because it happens only twice a year. People feel free to act as they otherwise wouldn't, to drink, sing, and dress-up in silly costumes, but they feel safe because they can trust in their environment; they know that the controls aren't gone for too long. Learning to live within limits is part of growing up. We all develop character when we know we're free to lose ourselves, just for a while, before returning to reality. It's a brilliant solution that helps to meet all facets of our needs!

Even I was letting go and living out a fantasy. In my own way, I was also experiencing a new part of myself. Here I sat, welcomed by people of my own tribe, who live in many ways apart from others in American society. They dress by their own modest codes. They limit their exposure to the outside world. They don't own televisions, go to the movies, or swim in public beaches. But today we came together. Minute by minute, we were bridging the invisible yet real gulf that so often sets people apart. Today we were as one.

Two hours passed in a heartbeat, but I was feeling more and more at home. Not only did the music sound more familiar but also my energy level, which had been flagging when we arrived, began to rise. Without a doubt, I was absorbing the positive energies of those in the room. I wasn't just eating a meal; I was being infused with spiritual nourishment as well. In the spirit of hidden miracles, many "angels" were helping me to feel more and more at home. Welcoming smiles and gestures, uplifting music, delicious food, hearty laughter, moving talks, and even the angel of a special blessing seemed to be just for me. I felt the warmth of everyone's figurative embrace.

The phone rang many times during dinner. One call was from Israel, where Rachel's son was studying. A parade of people took the receiver to exchange good wishes, with him and then with others who called. Blessings flowed back and forth across thousands of miles. I watched, amazed at all the connections being made. At one point, Rachael's son-in-law, filled with good food and wine, received a blessing from his father over the phone. And then he blessed me! "May you dance with a cane at your great-grandchildren's wedding!" he said. What an interesting image that created in my mind!

At times, the dinner swirling around me seemed completely fragmented. The music, the phone calls, the singing seemed to be a jigsaw puzzle whose pieces were scattered on the floor. One by one, however, the pieces began to fit together.

In many ways, the people I sat with resisted many of the intrusions and innovations of modern, technological life; yet, they also embraced them. The phone brought them closer to their loved ones. The tape recorder playing in the background filled the house with traditional music. Together, my hosts and all their guests created an encompassing universe bringing us all together in mutual love and understanding.

And behind it all, always sustaining them, was the structure of the Torah. However chaotic the Seudah (celebration) seemed, the laughter, costumes, and drinking were all parts of a highly organized sit-down dinner. It had a clear beginning, middle, and end and was punctuated by many moments of thanks to God in the form of blessings bestowed on each other. All the silliness and gaiety was framed by short, dignified speeches called "d'vrai Torah". All the raucous behavior, no matter how fluid and loose, was always appropriate—no one swore, told off-color jokes, or resorted to sarcasm. Though the dining room vibrated and jiggled like a moving train, it was ultimately as steadfast as a rock.

I thought about the book written by Liz Harris about the Hassidic family. Each time she had tried to interview the husband, to get to know and understand him, he had been extremely hesitant to open up. He didn't want to talk about himself, his personal or work life, or what he did each day. It took her a while to figure out the cause of his reluctance. In part, she attributed it to the fact that he wasn't comfortable talking to any women outside his family, even though he'd agreed to be interviewed. But the larger, more interesting reason was that he thought of himself simply as part of the Jewish people. His overriding purpose in life was to lead a good life full of meaning, a life that brought humanity in general—and the Jewish people in particular—to a higher level. His personal, daily life was just not that relevant to him. What he cared about were the energy and support he gave to and received from his community.

What a contrast this was to how most of us think of our lives. As Americans, we're always defining ourselves and each other by our job titles, our addresses, our incomes, and our hobbies. But at the Purim Seudah, no one asked me what I did or how I spent my free time or what interested me. They simply chatted with me. And I felt blessed simply because we were all together. I was there to listen and learn. There was no final exam; I could just soak it all in. Shoulder to shoulder, our senses heightened and our hearts filled with passion, we shared the dining room table and made it tremble with all our combined energy.

There were even a few minutes when I lost track of myself. It wasn't scary; rather, I felt as if I had merged with everyone present and we were somehow one unit. This wasn't an unfamiliar experience. As a teenager, I'd gone to a camp for Reform Jews and had danced and sang and studied my way through five days. I remember how satisfied I felt to be part of a group larger than myself. I remember once dancing in a circle outside at night, under the moonlight. I had been so happy and felt so at one with nature, my new friends, and God. How lovely it was to rediscover that feeling at the Haberman's.

Ahhh, the sense of belonging, the sense of community, I thought to myself as I drove home under the glow of the full moon that night of Purim. It is so essential to feel a sense of belonging. Now when I yearn for that special feeling, I relax in the joyous knowledge that it will happen for me again soon. Out of the blue, as a special gift to me, a marvelous miracle had happened. In a stranger's home, a dining room had become my community. I'll never forget that trembling, vibrating dining room and the feeling of excitement as I pictured us all on a train together. Those feelings are more satisfying than anything else I can imagine.

Thank you, Mr. and Mrs. Haberman, for taking me into your home and letting the miracle happen. Thank you, Mr. Moon, for accompanying me home. With such good companions, how could life not be full and sweet and good?

Muse and Ponder

Take some time over the next few weeks to think about how community could work better for you. Imagine yourself as an architect of community development, that you are given free reign to decide how and where people should live. What decisions would you make?

Suppose, for example, that you feel totally burdened by having to tend to the household chores of shopping, cooking, and cleaning after a full day of work. What would you do, if you were in charge of your environment, to change your life for the better? Perhaps you'd imagine yourself in a beautiful home where you had a small kitchen for snacks and small meals, but instead of preparing and eating main meals there, you'd eat your meals in a communal dining hall where all you had to do was show up and sit down. You'd be served wonderful food, freeing you to talk with your family and others around you. Perhaps there would even be reclining chairs where you could catch up with neighbors over a leisurely cup of tea. Can you sense that this is one of my fantasies? Maybe it's yours, too. It's only natural that busy women might wish for a community that would serve their needs on a daily basis.

For the next few weeks, be inventive and imaginative and let your imagination run free. Then, a month or so from now, come back and re-read this story and your notes. Can you think of three practical changes you can make in your community that would create positive change for you, that would make your life more fulfilling and more emotionally healthy?

You may not be able to indulge in my fantasy communal meal, but perhaps you can decide to get together regularly with two or three other families, sharing a potluck dinner in each other's homes on a rotating basis. This way, you could have an easy, casual meal together, and everyone would get a chance to talk during dinner. Best of all, everyone would feel taken care of and experience an ongoing sense of community.

Those of you so inclined may wish to look into your own traditions and/or other traditions to see how they support and encourage joyful connections through the use of community. Whether you choose to work from an established tradition or to invent your own, I hope you will derive some satisfaction in coming closer to the sweetness of life we feel when we're filled with love and appreciation for good companions.

MAZELTOV TO YOU! AND ME!
I Have a Job to Do – To Provide Joy!

Once you have a job to do, everything falls into place. At least that's the way it is for me. If I just have time on my hands with no particular purpose in mind, then the demons set in. Sometimes a host of characters come out to remind me of my failings, what I should have done, what I could have done. At other times I find myself in the middle of a familiar internal drama, experiencing feelings of loss, blame, and disappointment that I've had my whole life.

A while back, receiving an invitation to my cousin's wedding in California evoked an uncomfortable inner drama. What set me off was realizing that I didn't have any real reason to attend that I could think of. I was just one of many relatives; I didn't see myself as essential. That fact kept me from feeling entitled to spend the money needed to go to California, cancel an Enchanted Self workshop already scheduled for that weekend, cancel clients, etc. Sure, I'd see some cousins and we'd have the opportunity to spend a happy day together, but I saw most of these cousins frequently at other occasions, closer to home.

Yet something nagged at me I really felt bad! Again and again I almost canceled my workshop. I wouldn't understand why for several years, until I attended another wedding, a religious one.

The most shocking moment occurred immediately, as soon as I walked through the door. Complete strangers stopped me and said, "Mazel Tov!" (May your stars be lined up in your favor!).

I couldn't understand it. They didn't know me. I didn't know them. I barely knew the people who were getting married. In fact, I had come to the wedding as a courtesy and to experience what a religious ceremony was like. "Mazel Tov," I forced myself to say back because it seemed the polite thing to do, even though I felt almost affronted and even a little offended to be addressed so almost personally by strangers.

Later, when I described this experience to a friend who was religious, she smiled. "The celebration was for all of you," she explained. We're all connected; one person's happiness is another person's happiness, just as one person's tragedy is another person's tragedy."

I didn't need to know the bride and groom well to be part of their shared milestone. Just by attending, I was acknowledging that a good thing was happening in my community and therefore to me, and so I deserved to be congratulated. I wasn't simply an invited guest, but an active participant—a member of the community celebrating together.

What a profound insight! This is a very different orientation from the one I grew up with. Thanks to her explanation, I came to see the way I had been greeted as an affirmation of ties that connect us to each other. I also saw immediately why I had fretted so over my cousin's wedding years before! My heart had known what my mind couldn't get itself around at the time: I was essential! What an indescribably warming thought.

After the ceremony, the band began playing. It was time to dance. The women took their places on the women's side of the hall, while the men gathered behind a barrier on the other side. I usually enjoy dancing and was eager to join in, but I was also anxious. At most weddings and Bar Mitzvahs, this is when I'd experience anxiety in the pit of my stomach, a queasy uneasiness. As the circle began to form, I'd stand with the others, wanting so much to let myself go and join in while worrying that I wasn't a part of things. That's when the old demons visited me, the ones who say, "Take a good look at yourself—you're too fat, you're too old, and you're trying too hard. Who's going to invite you to join in the dancing with them? Who would want to? Look, they all know each other much better they than know you. Look how much fun they're having. Look how awkward you feel. It's always been this way, since you were a little girl, the same old story. Some people just don't luck out. You never have and you never will."

Yet at this wedding, where I knew virtually no one, I was remarkably free from this anxiety. Though I expected them, the demons never arrived. Instead, I felt totally at ease and confidant that, no matter what I did, I wouldn't be rejected, and indeed I wasn't. The women welcomed me. Whenever I broke into the circle, I was given a helping hand and accepted in a very companionable way. We danced for a dizzying 40 minutes, then 50, without a break. And with each passing moment, I felt more and more connected to everyone else in the circle.

In fact, I felt so close to the other women that, when I looked over to their side, I was almost shocked to see the men there. "Oh yes," I had to remind myself, "they are here too, those MALES. They're so different from us, so harsh and manly; they move with such ferocious energy. They're nothing like us..." It wasn't that they repulsed me so much as that I had no desire to be with them. Nothing about them could seduce me to leave the circle of women enfolding me. I was simply in my own place with my own kind, and I felt so good. I danced and danced, the good feelings growing inside me, until I felt as if I were incubating pleasantness.

The separate dancing and the feelings of pleasure generated by this wedding began to work their magic. I began to realize that I was at this wedding not simply because I was invited but because I had a purpose. And my purpose was to feel joyful. As I said before, having a clear purpose is like receiving a gift from the Great Divine. With purpose and focus, I'm sure of myself. I'm not intimidated or embarrassed; I feel strong. I know things will work out even if I don't know exactly how, and I'm imbued with a strong sense of my own dignity and status in life.

Recently I had the opportunity to hear a woman lecture about marriage. "Look at how joyful and full of joy (freilich, Yiddish for joy) a bride is," she said. "On that day, you see the happiness of her connection to God, to the intent of her life, to her future husband. She's full of life. We are most happy when we're connected. What makes us sad is that we see the shadow, not the whole picture. The Hassidic way of teaching helps us to see the light. The light is connection. The light is the joy that comes with connection, with the intent of connection."

"When you're not plugged in," another woman commented, "the motor doesn't work."

Last night I went to Borough Park for the wedding of a fellow whom I had never met. I barely know his mother, who is the neighbor of a good friend of mine. But I was included, and I was thrilled. I went to the wedding with a purpose. My assignment was to help provide joy, to help elevate all of us through the experience of joy. I didn't really need to know anyone else that well; I had a part to play, and I played it. I congratulated, smiled, and transmitted as much warmth and blessings as I could to all around me. At the same time, I became infused with those feelings.

My personal "joy" infusion came during the dancing. I've learned that you have to dance for more than a few minutes to experience a "vibrational high." Maybe teenagers know this instinctively, and that's why they dance for hours at a time. Yet we seem to forget this as we grow older. At this wedding, I remembered. I stayed on the dance floor for ten, fifteen, twenty minutes. The time flew by. I began to feel relaxed, high, and alive all at once. The infusion was working.

Full of renewed energy, I could have clicked my heels as I left the party at the evening's end. I drove home refreshed and uplifted. It's a great feeling to connect and belong. There's no way that we can become "plugged in" without becoming more charitable and kinder, without honing our ability to listen, to focus, to be there for others, and to be there for ourselves. We need to be the kind of people whose motors are always running.

May we all find joyous ways to have purpose, plugged in to life so that our motors are running, set on "Joy".

Personal Assignment

Imagine taking on a personal assignment to provide joy in at least three different settings. For example, you might take on the assignment of special birthday treats for every seven-year-old in your town.

What would your assignments be?

How would you do them?

Let your imagination run wild. Money, energy, time are of no concern to you. All you need to do is figure out how you will "plug in" to joy, and share it!

Let this be a fun assignment. Don't fret or worry. Ways of bringing yourself back to practical implementation will emerge over time. I promise they will!

A CHANUKAH TREAT
Lights My Way Home!

"Come, we'll be lighting the candles!" Malkie Diamondstone's radiant voice came through the telephone lines with a warmth that I could almost feel. "Yes of course I'd love to be with you," I said. "See you Thursday at around 5:30."

For several years, I had been going to Malkie's for at least one night of the Chanukah Festival. Varying numbers of children were always there, sometimes seven, eight, and even ten. On this occasion, the guest list was modest, only Malkie's four youngest daughters, but we also had the delight of hearing, via cell phone, from her daughter who is studying in Israel.

Mr. Diamondstone, looking distinguished in his special black coat and black hat, placed the menorah in the window near the front door so that all who passed could see the lights. It was an oil menorah, with each of eight little cups holding liquid oil and wicks. An oil menorah is a lovely idea— much more authentic than a menorah with wax candles. After all, one of the "miracles" of Chanukah is that oil, not a wax candle, burned for eight days when there was only enough left for one day.

After the menorah was lit, we sat in the front hall on folding chairs so that we could look at the Menorah and watch the little flames. The family, including Dafnia in

Jerusalem, recited prayers and various psalms and sang songs in honor of Chanukah. Listening to their strong, melodic voices and feeling the passion pass through the room, I felt truly inspired.

I was amazed to hear Dafnia's voice come through on the speakerphone. Like a physics lab, it demonstrated to me that sound really does take time to travel: Dafnia was always just a little bit behind, finishing a beat later than her sisters and her parents, which made perfect sense—after all, her voice had to travel seven thousand miles! Hearing her sing with her family across all that distance was truly a modern miracle. I felt as if I were witnessing one of those golden moments when a fairly new invention is used for the common good!

How beautiful, I thought to myself, that this family was making such an effort to stay together even across all those miles! Those of Malkie's daughters who weren't in the house were celebrating the holiday with other family members. Although Dafnia couldn't be with us physically, she just had to join in anyway!

Finally the singing ended. Someone switched off the lights in the front hallway. The menorah flickered in the darkness, for all who walked or drove by to see, a testament to the will to overcome the darkness.

All at once, the family bustled to life once more. The hungry, restless children started teasing and tussling with each other; while Malkie put out snacks and a discussion arose about what to wear, since they had all been invited to a family party. Mr. Diamondstone left the room to go to his study, and the cell phone was put away. Suddenly it was just another busy night in the life of a big, busy family.

But for me, those 45 minutes of radiant singing sitting in the midst of this family would hang on much longer—in fact, it lit my entire way home!

Ponderings

Have you ever visited someone and gone home with the positive energy you have felt in their home lighting your way home? Take some time to reminisce. What was it that they offered? Would you like to experience it again?

How could you bring similar positive energies into your world so that others are bathed in your light?

SHABBOS
The Greatest Gift of All

Sometimes when we visited my mother-in-law, Lillian Holstein, she would reminisce about growing up in New York City's Lower East Side. She said that she would never forget walking home before Shabbos, on Friday afternoons, and smelling the fragrant aromas of chicken soup and other savory delights wafting from every window. When she came to her own small apartment building and climbed the stairs to her family's flat, she knew just what smells to expect at every floor—Mrs. Cohen's stuffed cabbage, which she baked faithfully every week, and Mrs. Karinski's fresh apple strudel, which she painstakingly prepared for her son.

But best of all were the aromas that came from her very own apartment, where her mother, Rose, was busily preparing the traditional fresh challah, chicken soup and chicken roast, mandel bread, and a variety of other treats that changed week to week. The sparse apartment had been cleaned to spotlessness, and newspapers lined the small foyer to remind people to take off their shoes so as not to spoil the newly washed floor. After all, it was almost Shabbos!

Lillian loved to talk about this weekly experience. Occasionally I wondered how she could get so much pleasure from remembering a holiday she herself no longer observed. My family never observed Shabbos. In our house in Connecticut's suburban Fairfield County, Saturday was just Saturday, a day to do errands or have fun. Sure, I was confirmed. For three years, coinciding with the years I spent in junior high school, my mother dropped me off at Temple Beth El each Saturday morning so I could attend morning services. I enjoyed them—though I have to admit that my enjoyment was heightened by laughs and giggles and secret discussions in the hallways and bathroom. I never thought about my mother not coming in with me: she simply didn't, and I didn't expect her to.

After I was confirmed, I spent my Saturday mornings playing violin as a member of the Norwalk Community Symphony Youth Orchestra. I was in high school then, and I spent my afternoons at football games, shopping at Loehman's, or preparing for a date.

Some Saturday afternoons, though, we went to visit my Babu (my father's mother) in New Haven. My father carefully instructed me to not touch the lights, either to turn them on or off, since this was forbidden during Shabbos, which Babu strictly observed. Babu also never wrote or drove on Shabbos. She seemed like a relic from the past. In some vague way I knew we had to honor her, but I had no idea what Shabbos meant or that it belonged to us. It "belonged" to my Babu because she was old fashioned; it had nothing to do with me.

Over years, Saturdays gradually took on other meanings. Married, a mother, and a therapist, I'd spend Saturdays working in the office, seeing patients with my husband, going to my kids' basketball and baseball games, catching up on extra cooking, or shopping, on occasion.

But often, come Saturday, I'd find myself in a sour mood. I never felt eager to go to the mall or the grocery store. If I worked in the morning, I felt frazzled and high-strung by mid-afternoon. Did I know what I was missing? Absolutely not. I was only aware that the weekend was often not a blessed relief, but instead seemed to intensify some of my worst moods. Why did I succumb to these bad moods, I wondered. Did I have issues that were unresolved? Sometimes I thought that maybe I was lonely, that I missed a more encompassing sense of family and community. I resigned myself to my periodic dark moods.

My weekend adventure in the Amish Country, as a guest of Mrs. Olson and her family on their Mennonite farm, changed all my assumptions. If she had found a way to exist within her ancient tradition—to live in the present but enfolded in a kind of living past—then why couldn't I? Suddenly it was so clear to me. I needed to experience a more authentic Judaism, a Judaism that smelled both of the old days and the old ways. If I could do that, I'd learn something that I didn't know just yet. I didn't know <u>what</u> I'd learn, but I felt the urge to seek it out.

The question was, How could I get there? How could I connect with my "tribe", even if only for a weekend?

One day I was chatting with my cousin about our approaching birthdays. We often shared our thoughts on aging and tried to think of special ways to celebrate our birthdays together. I was trying to describe my recent desire to taste authentic Judaism.

"Why don't we meet in Lakewood?" she asked. (Lakewood is a very orthodox community.) She suggested that we stay with a friend of hers, where I'd be guaranteed to sample a rich slice of authentic Judaism, since the woman observed customs that went back hundreds, if not thousands, of years. My cousin didn't have to convince me any further. My bag, figuratively speaking, was already packed.

When the fall day arrived, however, and I was driving to Lakewood, I felt my heart pounding. I was both scared and excited, feeling that I was about to pass into another space, another world.

Ruth, our hostess, had given me directions to Twelfth Street, which I found easily enough—but which was her house? I drove a bit until I saw a girl, about seven years old, sitting on the outdoor steps. As I drove by, she made eye contact with me and waved her hand. She seemed to be a lighthouse, guiding me home.

I walked into the house to find everything in a state of disarray. Shabbos was only 45 minutes away, and there was still a lot to be done. Ruth, a beautiful woman with an engaging smile and piercing blue eyes, gave me a hug, sent one of her daughters down for my suitcase, and whisked me into the kitchen so I could join my cousin, who had arrived earlier. She offered me a seat at the table and asked whether I'd like tea or coffee and a slice of cake or a piece of strudel. She wouldn't take no for an answer. I, of course, obliged, delighting in the comfort of this late-afternoon snack.

The children raced around like whirlwinds, putting coins in the charity box, asking Ruth questions about their clothing, drying their hair, and, at the very last minute, tidying up in the kitchen. The floor was swept one last time, knobs on the stove were turned to "off", and suddenly, as if by magic, Shabbos entered.

In the dining room sterling silver candlesticks took up nearly half the large table. Everyone lit a candle to welcome Shabbos, including Ruth's children: five boys and five girls. We watched the candles glow in the semi-darkness. (The family had lit several lamps that would stay on throughout the night and day.)

Ruth's husband, Rabbi Saunders, soon left for shul (Yiddish word for synagogue) with his sons; Ruth and her daughters stayed at home to pray. Unfamiliar with the prayer, I studied the interesting books in Ruth's living room and felt myself unwinding totally. Indescribable peace and serenity began seeping into me. It was hard to believe that the family went through this elaborate ritual every weekend.

Shabbos dinner took place in Ruth's beautiful dining room, at a long table set for all the children and guests. (In addition to my cousin and me, several of Ruth's nieces from Brooklyn had arrived.) Like a head of state, Rabbi Sanders sat at the head of the table, presiding over the elegant, moving, yet hamish(easy and familiar) meal, chanting traditional blessings over the bread and wine. Not knowing what to do, I simply "followed the leader", getting up to wash my hands ritually, participating as well as I could. During the meal Rabbi Sanders gave a short talk about the Torah portion of the week (traditionally Jews read the same section of the Torah, the same week every week) and engaged my cousin and me in conversation. He was gracious but formal at the same time, calling us by our last names.

I could see that the children were beginning to get restless, but they channeled their energy into clearing the table and bringing in new platters of food. Though they ran around, there was still perfect order. Probably the most moving part of the dinner was listening to the children sing with their father. The oldest child was 19 and the youngest 2, and though their voices ranged in power and vibrancy, they all sounded like angels. The sweet melodies penetrated my soul and brought tears to my eyes.

I knew that if my dad could have been there, he would also have been crying—he would have recognized, as I did, that something from long ago, across the ocean, from the old country, had come alive in the Sanders' dining room. Their rituals and the sounds of their voices touched something old and tribal in me. It was almost a call of the wild, a signal I would have known anywhere.

"Come home!" the voice cried.

"I'm here," I answered silently.

At that moment I knew that the nameless quality I'd been searching for really did exist. I thought of all the bad moods and discontent I'd endured during a lifetime of Saturdays, hundreds and hundreds of Saturdays, and realized what I'd been deprived of. Without realizing it, I'd been hungering for the soul food of spending Shabbos with my tribe. Though no one set out to cheat me, I felt cheated nonetheless.

That night my cousin and I chatted for hours about our children, our lives, and our feelings about Judaism. It was a wonderful, womanly chat, the kind of conversation in which every utterance spawns three or four simultaneous responses. Pleasantly exhausted, I finally went to bed wearing an eye mask I'd salvaged from an airplane trip. That was the only way I could shut out the light that had been left on in our bedroom, which would remain on until Shabbos was over.

The next day was pleasant and restorative . . . and too fleeting. The first of two highlights occurred during the afternoon, when some of Ruth's friends came over to meet my cousin and me. Five women sat down to talk in the living room—nothing remarkable about that. What was remarkable was that as we sat, fourteen children were in the same room with us. They played board games, chatted, and read, and yet we women were still able to talk. I couldn't fathom how these mothers had done it. The children weren't robots, yet they had clearly been raised to understand that space had to be shared and everyone in the room respected so that we could all do what we needed to do.

The other moment I'll always remember is when we came to the table for the third and last meal of Shabbos. This was a very important meal, Rabbi Sanders explained to me, a nostalgic meal. Shabbos is so special, so beloved—it's a heightened time when our souls expand, when our capacity for joy is enhanced and replenished, and when we feel a sense of closeness to those we love and to the great Divine—that those who observe it hate to see it go.

We ate a light meal of tuna fish, egg salad, and other cold dishes. A sense of poignancy hovered above us. With his children accompanying him, the Rabbi sang "nigumim" (wordless songs), most of which were in a mournful minor key. Music like this always evokes a sense of loss and melancholy. Once again, I found myself enraptured by the music, which was playing on my heartstrings. I watched the sun set with as much regret as I'd ever felt, as if I'd been celebrating Shabbos in this way for my whole life.

My first Shabbos weekend ended all too quickly. I knew as I drove away that I would find my way back one day soon, not only to Ruth's house, but to Shabbos.

How, I wondered, and why, had my family given up such a renewing weekly experience? Here was a wonderful opportunity to do something good for your health, for the sense of community, something we were commanded to do ... and yet we apparently had shed the commandment easily, like an old worn-out garment. I had to remind myself that, to immigrant Jews, Shabbos hadn't always been considered a treat. If a Jewish man told his employer that he was unable to work on Saturday because of religious reasons, even if he said that he could work on Sunday instead, when everyone else rested, it was likely that he would lose his job. How many people could afford to do that? No wonder observing Shabbos became less important.

In the past fifty years, however, things have changed. Most Jews are in a position to observe the Shabbos if they choose to—an observance that would bring pleasure, replenishment, and a sense of Jewish connection to their lives.

Ponderings

This leads me to pose some questions:

Why would we give up something so nourishing?

What kind of message does it send to the rest of the world when we trivialize a sacred opportunity that was specifically given to us as a people, which we were commanded to observe?

Do we have an obligation to live a Jewish life and to honor those Jews who died simply for being Jewish? Shouldn't we try to live the kind of life they were denied?

Aren't we obligated to teach the next generation the core tenets of our faith and tradition? As I understand it, Shabbos is even more important to Jews than the High Holy Days.

If I sound angry, it's because I am. Perhaps if my heart hadn't been aching for so many years before I found Shabbos, I could discuss the subject more calmly. But I feel I have been cheated out of the experience of Shabbos for so many years that it angers me to think how many people are, in so many ways and every day, cheating themselves out of the joy to which they are entitled.

We all pay a price for ignorance, a high price. Just as a child who never learns to read is at a huge disadvantage, a person pays a huge price for remaining ignorant of his or her tradition.

I hope that my impressions, recollections, thoughts, and questions leave you curious. May they spur you to have your own adventure and stimulate you to find your own path to connect with the traditions from your heritage or other traditions you have adopted or created, whether they are daily, weekly, or yearly. Whatever they are, grab onto them, and hold onto them for dear life. Then, teach them diligently to your children.

CHESED
What We All Need –
Acts of Loving Kindness

Listening to a learning tape, part of a series entitled "Attaining Happiness"* narrated by Rabbi Eschbel Schachter, I learned about Abraham, the first Jew. His most important personality characteristic, above all others, was kindness, or, in Hebrew, chesed. Thus, the notion of doing acts of kindness has come down through the Jewish people over thousands of years from generation to generation. It is taught as a major attribute of personality, style, and behavior.

The rabbi explained that chesed is not to be done without thought. For example, giving money to a young man so that he can buy drugs and further abuse himself is not an act of kindness. One must always use judgment, even in performing acts of kindness. However, chesed does not have to cost you money. You can just smile at someone or say "Hello." Sometimes that's enough to make the person's day. Just a twinkle in your eye or the warmth of your smile can create a world of difference.

I've heard so many stories about the power of chesed. Here are two very different ones. The first, none of us should ever experience, but it illustrates the heroic proportions that kindness can take.

A Jewish man who had been fighting in a war returned to his home to find that it had been vandalized and his family killed by a particular officer in the Lithuanian army. Incensed beyond reason, he grabbed his gun and went to the man's home.

Pushing open the door with the butt of his gun, he couldn't believe his eyes. There on the floor was his own rug, his own silver candlesticks were on the table, and every object he held dear was now in the officer's house. But the worst was yet to come: when he came upon the officer's family cowering in the kitchen, he saw that the officer's daughter was wearing one of his own daughter's skirts!

He aimed his gun and was just about to shoot when the little girl began to cry, "Please don't kill my father. Please don't kill my daddy."

In the midst of his own searing pain, the Jew felt the pain of this little girl. He lowered his hand, turned around, and left the house, unable to take his retribution.

Now, the next story seems less dramatic, but it is no less heroic! It comes from one of the Small Miracle books by Yitta Halberstam and Judith Leventhal in which they relate stories about Rabbi Carlbach of the Carlbach Synagogue on 79th Street in New York City.

Rabbi Carlbach, it seems, always made a point of writing down the names and phone numbers of people he met. He didn't just record their numbers, however. He would also call them, just to say hello.

One of the young men the rabbi had met was very depressed and had decided to end it all. He was going to hang himself in his bedroom. In the midst of preparing for this, the phone rang. He was surprised, since he was not expecting a call. In fact, he hadn't spoken to anyone for weeks.

For whatever reason, he stopped his gruesome proceedings and picked up the phone. He heard Rabbi Carlbach's booming voice saying, "Hello! We met a few weeks ago. I've been carrying around a piece of paper with your name and number on it, and I just thought I'd call to say how much I enjoyed meeting you!"

The young man didn't tell the rabbi that he was about to end his life, but neither did he hang up. He stayed on the line, and the two men exchanged words.

When the conversation was over, the young man sat on his bed. "Someone called me on the phone," he thought to himself. "Someone thought of me. I <u>exist</u>." Thinking about this, he realized that he no longer felt like taking his own life.

I know myself how exquisitely important this feeling is. A vivid memory comes to my mind.

It was Rosh Hashanah, the Jewish New Year, several years before I started my Judaic journeying. Quite unexpectedly, a woman I didn't know well (our daughters had gone to Hebrew school together) invited my family to her house for a light lunch after services. Since we usually spent the holidays by ourselves, we were all delighted to accept her invitation, even my husband and children. When we arrived, we realized that she had also invited many other people, but that didn't dim our happiness. Her house was lovely, the food delicious, and the company engrossing. It was a very special way to usher in the New Year.

The next year, as we had no plans, I secretly hoped that she'd invite us once again. In fact, I was preoccupied with this hope. However, as the days passed, no invitation arrived. After services, as everyone stood in the synagogue's foyer to wish everyone else a Happy New Year, I saw the woman. She saw me, too. She smiled and began to walk toward me. My heart was pounding; I was so relieved! Though it was at the last minute, she'd still invite us. We'd join others in a festive meal rather than return to our empty house by ourselves. What a relief! Maybe this would happen every year, and we'd have a lovely tradition to look forward to.

As the woman came closer, I prepared myself to accept her invitation. To my dismay, I soon realized that she hadn't seen me at all, because she was walking right by me. She didn't even say hello. Instead, she greeted a couple standing behind me.

I felt terrible. We went home alone. My kids didn't notice; they went out to play. I, on the other hand, cried for two hours. My husband knew that I was upset but didn't know why. How could I begin to explain how much I needed a simple act of kindness . . . that I had needed to feel included?

Of course, I could have felt satisfied just being with my own family, and I also could have invited people over to our house. The truth, however, was that I didn't know how to turn a holiday into a joyous occasion. My upbringing had not included demonstrations or lessons on how to do this. My background in Judaism was so shallow that it verged on the non-existent, but beside that, I had no idea how to develop the reservoir of emotional energy that I'd need to plan the kind of get-together that would warm my heart and raise my spirits. I needed help.

We all need help. We all have our frailties. That is what makes chesed such a beautiful concept. What if we all just assumed that no one is perfect, that we all occasionally need the comfort of a smile or a warm "hello", that we all need to have our spirits bolstered, to hear praise, to feel included. Yes, we all wish to be affirmed, to be able to say, "I exist!"

Chesed, a simple act of loving kindness, can do all that . . . and more.

Ponderings

Has anyone done an act of kindness to you or for you that really made a difference?

If money and time were no object, what are three acts of kindness that you would do during the next year?

Enjoy seeing yourself giving these gifts to the world.

Is there one act of kindness you can begin building right now, perhaps an easy one that you can definitely feel good about and consistently carry out?

* These tapes are produced by the Chofetz Chaim Heritage Foundation located in Monsey, New York.

SOUL SPARKS
I Get a Chance To Be in a Holy Place

In Judaism, there is a notion of sparks—Divine sparks—that are located in various parts of the world, within ourselves, and even in the atmosphere. For example, when we celebrate a holiday at a certain time of year, we tap into the sparks, or vibrational energies, that have accumulated throughout our lifetime of celebrating that particular holiday.

In the same way, we encounter sparks when we visit the holy resting places of great people such as Rachel, one of the matriarchs, or when we touch holy books such as the Torah. That is one of the reasons that Jews treat religious writings and objects of worship with loving care. This custom even extends to burying old, unusable prayer books. Recognizing that these are sacred items, we need to retire them with respect.

Did you know that a home can become a holy place? In fact, it is a Jewish woman's responsibility to make her home into a temple, a living sanctuary where all that's positive in life can unfold in a nourishing, nurturing, loving atmosphere.

I remember the afternoon, soon after beginning my own Judaic journey, that I first recognized the holiness of a Jewish home.

Here's what happened: My teenage son and I were supposed to deliver something to my friend Rachel Rosen at 2 p.m. She'd warned us that she might be a little late, and had told us to go in if they hadn't yet returned.

Her home, as my son and I soon discovered, consisted of the ground-floor apartment of a dilapidated three-family house. We knocked and , hearing no response, went inside. It was hardly sumptuous. The living/dining room contained a battered sofa; a large, worn old dining room table; six or seven chairs; and many bookcases filled with Jewish books. The kitchen was a chaotic collection of dinnerware, silverware, glasses, and non-perishable foods, as well as the debris of breakfast—all awaiting cleanup. Clearly this was a busy household with many children. But there were no curtains on the windows. No frills. No ornaments. On the walls were pictures of great Jewish sages as well as scraps of paper listing all the good deeds the children had performed.

My son and I looked at each other, unsure of what to do. I was sure he was thinking about his soccer practice coming up in a couple of hours. After a few moments he surprised me by saying, "Gee it's very relaxing here. Let's just sit a while."

I couldn't have agreed more. We sat down on the battered couch, relaxed, and enjoyed the peaceful surroundings. Within minutes we found ourselves involved in a deep, spiritual conversation—he asked some questions related to Mount Sinai and the giving of the Torah, and I answered as well as I could. Soon we were talking about Jewish notions of heaven. At some point I remember thinking how good it felt—and how unusual—to have this kind of long conversation with a teenage boy. The time just flew by.

This obviously was no ordinary apartment! Its walls had collected sparks of energy that radiated hope, love, and nourishing feelings. Moreover, since there were no curtains, nothing "pretty" or ornamental, I found I didn't need ornaments. I felt much happier being in a space that was devoted to authentic living—full of books, comfortable places to sit, tributes to children and sages, and the chaos of busy lives revealed in unfolded laundry and the remains of shared meals—than I would have felt looking at recognized works of art in a sterile, perfectly ordered room.

After about forty-five minutes, my son looked at his watch. "I just realized something," he said. "Chanie never showed up."

It was true: we'd sat in her living room and discovered its treasures without her! Together, my son and I had realized it was a sanctuary where we both felt relaxed and comfortable enough with each other to have a remarkably intense spiritual conversation.

"Well, what do you think?" I asked. "Should we leave?"

"I guess so," he said.

We got up almost wistfully and walked into the sunlight. The time in Chanie's living room was a real eye-opener for me. Before visiting her, I'd never realized how much atmosphere a home could contain. She may not have shown up, but her presence was everywhere. I'd seen sparks fly— and that had changed everything.

Ponderings

How can you make your home, or even a small part of it, a more sacred place? We could all put holy sparks in our home if we would take the time to clarify inside ourselves what will make our homes more pure and filled with light. Here are a couple of suggestions:

You might want to start with a corner or even just a shelf, refresh that area by cleaning it out, and then place there special, meaningful objects.

On the other hand, you may want to go through your home, a small area at a time, discarding what doesn't feel good any more and adding objects or plants that clearly feel right.

Don't forget: what is no longer right for you may be something that can benefit someone else. You may find yourself enjoying giving away items and doing a good deed at the same time.

EVERYONE ENJOYS A GOOD STORY –
A Fire in Harlem

Positive action is so important in living a Jewish life. The word "mitzvah" is used to describe a positive action, a good deed. From my vantage point as a psychologist and as a woman, I feel that we have the emotional and physical energies necessary for performing mitzvahs if we like ourselves and feel of value. Only when the physical and emotional merge energies can we summon the courage, inspiration, and perspiration to go forth and carry out good deeds. If we feel that our lives are meaningless, that nothing we do is of any importance (Nothing I do matters!), it's much harder to live a life of positive action.

Even for those of us with the energy for positive action, though, good deeds are often hard to undertake. We, too, end up wondering if what we do has any meaning or importance. Sometimes we go out of our way to phone a difficult aunt, return a book, or give a compliment, and receive nothing in return. It's as if we're throwing sand into the wind. There's no feedback—no gesture of thanks. Nothing. So once again, we can be left feeling empty, even though we have behaved in a positive fashion. After all, while we should not be doing a good deed in expectation of a thank you, it's still nice to know that our efforts have had some sort of positive effect.

Wouldn't it be wonderful if we were rewarded every time we took a positive action? I can almost imagine being hugged and congratulated from on high. How good it would feel!

Yet in Judaism, our sages do not promise us that we will be instantly rewarded for our good deeds. We may not be rewarded at all as far as we can see. We are, however, assured that our good deeds have a positive benefit, whether we are aware of it or not. I like this concept, because I believe that we often underestimate both ourselves and the profound effect we can have on other people and events.

I know this to be true in my work as a psychologist. Sometimes clients tell me about a friend who is always smiling, always beaming, and how good she makes everyone feel. When I suggest my client can also make other people feel good by smiling, she insists that she's hardly visible, that it would make no difference to anyone if she smiled. She is unable to envision herself as someone who can influence others—yet clearly, she is! She has powers she knows nothing about.

This story will illustrate my point. I heard it on Tisha B'Av, a Jewish fast day, when a renowned English rabbi spoke at a local synagogue. Though I didn't take notes, here is the essence of his account.

The Rabbi began his talk by declaring that doing good deeds is like hitting tennis balls over a fence so high that you can't see what's on the other side. Sometimes a ball comes back to you. You don't know if it's your ball or someone else's, for you have no idea where your own balls have landed. What's more, you will never know the score! All you can do is practice your form and hope that you are improving.

The principle is the same when it comes to doing good deeds. We operate blindly. We don't know where good deeds will land, whom they will affect, or how. But it's important to keep on performing them. He then told this story:

One day, many years ago, an African-American man happened to be walking through Harlem when he came upon a horrible scene: a small apartment building was burning. Flames were shooting into the sky. He saw three children standing in the window of a second floor apartment, next to a fire escape. Panicked, they were too afraid to move. People stood on the sidewalk, in as much shock as the children and just as immobile. The man knew that he had to help the children.

He found some rags, wet them in a puddle in the gutter, and climbed the fire escape to the window. He reassured the panicking children and encouraged them until they came foreword. When they were close enough, he grabbed them one by one, draped rags around their mouths, and brought them down the fire escape.

At that moment, the children's distraught parents came running down the street, filled with horror as they saw their building on fire. Finding their children and quickly realizing that they were safe and unharmed, they thanked the stranger profusely. "You saved our children's lives," they said. ""How can we ever repay you?"

"I did what anyone would do," the man said.

Years later there was an international crisis over the fate of Ethiopian Jews. The difficult and corrupt president of Ethiopia had been demanding millions of dollars to free the 12,000 remaining Jews and let them fly to Israel. However, he had recently added a new demand: he wanted President George W. H. Bush to call him, personally.

President Bush's cabinet met to decide what to do. They didn't want to accede to a tyrant's wishes, but to not make the phone call would condemn innocent people to death. The first vote ended in a tie. To break the deadlock, they turned to the one person who hadn't yet voted—a distinguished, middle-aged African-American.

When asked how he would vote, he said, "Years ago, an Ethiopian Jew saved me from a fire in my house. When my parents thanked him and tried to repay him, he said, 'I did what anyone would do. I did a mitzvah.' I think I now understand the meaning of the world 'mitzvah', and I will cast my vote in favor of making the phone call." President Bush phoned, and 12,000 Jews were on their way to freedom!

See how much difference one person can make? Our most ordinary actions can have extraordinary repercussions!

When I left the synagogue, my body was hungry, but my soul was nourished.

Reflections

Take a few moments to reminisce about positive actions that you or others have taken. Remember, a positive action can be very small and even disguised. For example, just being courteous rather than indifferent or rude can turn into a good deed. The recipient of your courtesy may be strengthened in ways you will never know. It happened to me when Mrs. Johnson, my third grade teacher, put some extra effort into trying to teach me to read.

When I was in the third grade, I could hardly read because I had undiagnosed dyslexia. Frustrated because I was unable to keep up with even the lowest reading group, I felt a sense of dread each time the teacher asked us to take out our reading books. One day Mrs. Johnson called me up to her desk and said, "Barbara, I see you're having a lot of trouble reading, and I have a suggestion. You're a smart little girl with a good memory. Why don't you stop trying to sound out words and instead simply memorize them? Soon you'll know hundreds and then thousands of words by sight, and by the time you finish the third grade, you will be a very good reader—I promise you."

Her words inspired me, giving me the courage and confidence I needed to learn to read. Actually, I'd been trying her approach in secret, but her permission, combined with my eagerness to please her, gave me a burst of energy. By the end of the school year, I had memorized so many words by sight that I won the prize for having read the most library books.

I don't know if Mrs. Johnson realized what a profound effect her efforts with me had. She hit a tennis ball that led not only to my becoming an avid reader but to my feeling comfortable the rest of my life in the world of books.

Positive actions make great stories. After you finish musing, think about sharing with your family or friends your memories about positive actions taken by yourself or others. Your stories are sure to spark their memories also. Before you know it, good feelings along with good stories will be flying—just like those tennis balls.

MORE MUSINGS
Pleasure –
Ah! What a Delight ...

Pleasure—what a delightful concept! We all yearn for it, we all want more of it, and yet far too often the sense of elation, playfulness, and joy of pleasure eludes us. It's even hard for us to hang onto the more modest notion of having "peace of mind".

We stumble and struggle with this for a host of reasons. For one thing, we're often taught that we don't deserve pleasure. We've been bad; we didn't do something right, and now we've lost our chance forever. That's it! The opportunity has come and gone.

Many of us grew up hearing such negative messages. They were often said innocently enough, yet the moments when we heard these comments became crystallized in time, and they come back to haunt us when evoked in our present, tense lives. In other words, we've internalized these memories; they've become part of us, restricting us and cutting us off from joy. That's why, on many occasions, we become our own worst censors, keeping ourselves from the good moods to which we're so entitled.

On other occasions, life is just plain difficult. We hope for a full plate, and we feel disappointed when the plate looks half-empty. A woman who longs to find her soul mate remains single into middle age; another woman is cruelly and suddenly widowed at a young age. For other people, jobs go sour and necessitate that the family relocate; health problems arise; children turn difficult. Events like these invade our being, violating our private sense that we are capable of happiness, that we are supposed to enjoy peace of mind.

As I mentioned in my introduction, my actual "Aha!" moment—the moment that gave birth to my Enchanted Self work—occurred when I realized that women are marvelous. We are true survivors, not only in the practical sense but emotionally as well. Somehow, despite all we have to do, we manage to find ways to simply feel good, feel whole, and let our pleasure shine through.

The Jewish point of view, as I discovered in my journey, supports all of the above. Judaism assumes that we are entitled to pleasure and that it, in itself, is very important. Why? For two major reasons.

The first is very simple. A happy, thriving person can undertake positive actions, do good deeds, and be available—for others and for the world. A sad person, one who does not feel energized by her life experiences, will withdraw. Because she needs to spend most of her energy controlling and containing dark and angry emotions, she is able to accomplish only a minimal amount of good.

The second reason that Judaism supports joy and happiness is connected to the notion of the messianic age still to come. Practicing pleasure and states of joy help us to prepare ourselves for a better world, a world in which there will be no darkness and no evil. At the same time, our souls yearn for that blissful state that we can discover only in the hereafter. According to the mystic tradition in Judaism, the more we practice achieving these states while we're living on earth, the more accessible they will be to us after our souls depart our bodies.

As I've said often to my clients, it takes the same amount of energy to achieve a state of personal well-being that gives pleasure as it does to cultivate feeling miserable. Either always takes practice! How much better it is to practice experiencing pleasure than pain.

I'M WALKING OUT BACKWARDS
To Savor Every Moment

Once again, I'm leaving. This time I'm leaving the Chabad Rabbi's beautiful Victorian home in San Francisco. My stomach is replete with a delicious Shabbos lunch. My spirit is overflowing with the beauty of the Saturday services. I glow as I walk the four miles back to the hotel; how could I not be happy? I've just spent a morning with people who were truly interested in getting to know me. Several were psychologists like myself, in town for the American Psychological Association meetings. Our group was a medley of interesting lay people and professionals, gathered by the spiritual link of our Jewish day of rest.

I was delighted to have a chance to get to know everyone. During the Rabbi's interesting "Dvar Torah," a short talk usually tied into the Torah portion of the week, I felt connected and at peace, mentally stimulated and wanted, although I had never met my tablemates before today.

The Jewish sages say that on Shabbos you get a second soul that helps you to connect with the best that this world has to offer, along with a bit of the beauty of the world to come. Perhaps this was what created my additional capacity to experience the joy and connection with others that I felt as I sat at the table. Whatever it was, I greedily wanted more of it.

During and after the meal, we listened to beautiful "nigumim" (wordless melodies) that have come down through the ages, often representing a particular "shtetel" (Jewish village from Eastern Europe) or a particular branch of Jewish tradition such as Hasidism. The melodies are mostly melancholic, linking the soul with lost shtetels and with people long gone. My dad, who seldom consciously incorporated Jewish tradition into his daily life, always shed a tear when he heard these old melodies. At this particular Shabbos table, only the men sang, but I did not find it uncomfortable. I tapped my fingers on the beautiful linen tablecloth and tried to absorb the essence of each melody.

Before this particular lunch, I had relaxed in the front living room, looking at books and daydreaming as I gazed out the window. We were soon ushered into the dining room, where the Rabbi intoned the "Kiddush" (prayer before eating). After the Kiddush, we lined up to ritually wash our hands in the kitchen. This washing and reciting of prayers is one of the mitzvahs performed before eating bread or, in essence, any meal other than a snack.

Like many traditional aspects of Judaism, this one had seemed strange to me when I first experienced it. What was that pitcher, for instance, sitting near the sink, and why were people using it to pour water over their hands? Why wouldn't anyone respond to me when I asked this question?

Only later did I learn that silence after washing is part of the ritual, and, after I had experienced this ritual a few times, it took on a life of its own and began to make sense. The point is not simply to cleanse your hands, but to engage in a spiritual purification. I soon grew to enjoy this lining up with others and waiting, the silence of the table broken only by giggles and the effort to communicate without talking, using grunts, groans, eye movements, and hand gestures. All of this proved to be an extra level of fun and connection with my Shabbos companions.

While waiting my turn, I had a chance to glance around the Rebbitzin's kitchen. I loved the room, and during the meal I helped to carry dishes in and out of the dining room, just to be able to spend a few extra moments in the kitchen.

What was special about that room? Why did I feel that being there was a holy experience? It was stark and plain—no wallpaper, pictures, knickknacks, or pottery—just white walls adorned with a Jewish calendar. The woodwork was only moderately clean, suggesting the patting of lots of almost-clean little hands. It contained an industrial-sized refrigerator, an oversized old stove, and a giant urn of hot water. Large trays of food covered with tin foil were warming over a very, very low heat, on a part of the stove that had an aluminum cover called a "blech". The low flame under the blech is permitted as long as the heat remains constant, neither being turned higher nor lower, from the onset of Shabbos until after sundown on Saturday.

The kitchen itself seemed as if it had absorbed positive energy over the years. It seemed almost as if the walls were laughing gently and the floorboards reverberated with the chatter of countless happy little feet. I could sense years and years of accumulated vapors of good home cooking, providing comfort and joy, a sense of stability and the belief that anyone could find nurture there and that there would be plenty of food, no matter how many people shared the meal. It was as if the walls themselves could expand to make the necessary room. It was a magic kitchen, an Enchanted Kitchen. How could I not feel good—both yummy in my tummy and healthy in my heart and soul?

Eventually, however, I had to leave and return to my own life. As I said, "Farewell," and started walking the miles back to my hotel, I found myself processing my own traditions with fresh eyes and entertaining the notion that this tradition could hold nourishment and provide a safe haven for me. It was as if a breath of fresh air had blown inside my head. I could now see how the traditions of my religion could provide me with a sense of stability, continuity, and belonging.

A few years ago I heard a commentary on public radio, by a young Jewish man who often spent time with a famous Rebbe in the heart of Borough Park, Brooklyn. Although the young man still lived in Manhattan, worked, went to concerts, and dated there, he felt as if he belonged at least in part to the Rebbe's world. "Although I always leave the Rebbe," he said near the end of the broadcast, "I find myself walking away backward."

I resonated to this man immediately. I knew what he meant. Sometimes I have had to leave behind opportunities that I was not able to embrace at that time of my life, but I never fully leave in spirit. I remain in awe of the experience I've left behind, and I know the power of what they are offering. I come back as often as I can, both in reality and in my mind's eye.

That's exactly how I felt leaving the Shabbos I attended in the midst of the American Psychological Association convention. The living reality of my Jewish self had finally merged within me, incorporating my external flesh with my internal soul.

That day in San Francisco brought together many years of journeying for me, both as a positive psychologist and as a Jewish woman. In just one day, I had experienced true joy. I felt good about myself, knew myself better, had met my own needs, and felt part of both my major communities: psychology and Judaism.

I felt more able to share and to care about others. I realized that many of my positive feelings about the day and myself were made possible by the Rabbi and his Rebbetzein. They had opened their house to us and shared the positive energy that it contained, for they had turned their home into a true temple, a sacred place. Because of them, another Shabbos of delight had taken place.

How far I had come from my soul's cry for I knew not what after visiting the Mennonite farm! During the past ten years, I have traveled back and forth in time and space into my Judaic heritage. I have seen customs that I hadn't known existed and been aroused by feelings I didn't know I had; I have found new ways to put meaning into my life and my life's work, and I have made new friends and experienced holy places in ordinary living rooms and in simple kitchens. I've had a chance to make up for lost time and to connect to the Divine in new ways that felt right for me, for I have been immersed in pure water, spirit, song, dance, friendships, and learning.

Time has passed more rapidly than I would have liked it to over the past ten years, and yet I have been given the gift of a day of delight every week. I have been given the tools and the spirit to live an enchanting, Jewish life.

I have come home to a part of me lost long ago. Mentally I stretch lazily, like a pampered cat in a warm room, at peace with others and especially with myself. The hole in my heart has been mended, and enchantment surrounds me.

Reflections

We have metaphorically walked "hand in hand" through this book. It is up to you to continue from this point. Take your gift, your birthright to live a life of Delight. Continue to find the nourishment you need for your soul, travel your roads, climb your mountains, sing your songs, and immerse yourself in your own pure waters. And above all, be the beautiful person of mind, body, and spirit that you are.

My blessings and best wishes accompany you on your journey!

~*~*~*~

I would be very happy if you would share your journey by writing to me at _DrBarbara@EnchantedSelf.com_, _encself@aol.com_ or by joining me on my web site _www. enchantedself.com._

Sincerely,
Barbara

ABOUT THE AUTHOR

Dr. Barbara Becker Holstein is a nationally known leader in Positive Psychology. Her first book, *THE ENCHANTED SELF, A POSITIVE THERAPY*, challenges outdated psychological behaviors and attitudes. It shows clinicians and the public how to recognize what is right about each of us, rather than what is wrong. Her emphasis on positive memory retrieval has profoundly changed the focus of the treatment room. Now we can joyfully reclaim our talents and lost potential, even from a dysfunctional past.

This book was followed by *RECIPES FOR ENCHANTMENT, The Secret Ingredient is YOU!*, which combines stories for the heart and soul with follow-up activities and journaling. Dr. Holstein is now pleased to present her third book, **DELIGHT**, for your reading pleasure.

All of Dr. Holstein's books may be found at all major web book sites, and of course at www.enchantedself.com.

Joy and discovering our purpose in life are essential to Dr. Holstein's teachings. She educates the public in ways to increase the joy in one's life, sharing her knowledge with the public via her constant radio, audio, and television appearances. Listen to her 24/7 on www.ladybuglive.com.

sign up for her free e-mail newsletter, Enchantment in an E-mail, which reaches thousands by going to www. enchantedself.com.

Dr. Becker Holstein's web site, www.enchantedself. com, is full of good news, wonderful books and products, and other inspiring learning opportunities for women. Her teaching articles and uplifting stories flood the Internet, appearing on over 100 sites.

Dr. Becker Holstein knows that practice is essential in order to live a life of joy and meaning. In **DELIGHT**, she uses each story as a springboard for enticing the reader to get in touch with her own passions, unique gifts, and essence. You can reach Dr. Holstein at (877) B-JOYFUL. Her web site is www.enchantedself.com, and her e-mail address is encself@aol.com. She is available for media interviews, retreats, teleconferences, tele-classes, seminars, mind-body workshops, lectures, and coaching.